HERE AND THERE
IN ASTROLOGY

and

WHAT IS THE NATURE
OF THIS EVENT?

*

By IVY M. GOLDSTEIN-JACOBSON

*

Member of

AMERICAN FEDERATION OF ASTROLOGERS

and

FIRST TEMPLE & COLLEGE OF ASTROLOGY

at LOS ANGELES

All engravings by Marge J. Zander

Author of

Mathematics of the Astrological Chart
Foundation of the Astrological Chart
Simplified Horary Astrology
The Dark Moon Lilith in Astrology
All Over the Earth Astrologically
The Turn of a Lifetime Astrologically

Photographed from Mrs. Jacobson's typing
and
Printed in the United States
by
Pasadena Lithographers
Pasadena, California

* * * * * *

The Oncoming Separative Aspect

To L.R.J., In Memoriam

In case I never see your face again -
  (For who can say, at such a time as this?)
In case I never take your hand again
  Or know the blessing of your goodnight kiss,
Let me embrace you now, with brimming heart
  Speaking the words I want your heart to hear:
You are the meaning of all life to me,
  You are the darling of my heart, most dear.

Now do we recognize that time is sweet,
  Based on our coming loss: for who shall say
What is to happen in the home or street?
  Let it be heaven now, though but a day.
Let it be glorious and outspoken gain,
  Let us once more embrace and laugh and kiss,
In case I never see your face again -
  (For who can say, at such a time as this?)

* * * * * *

Table of Contents

* * * * *

Introduction

Part One

The first part of this book is comprised of special sections designed to give the student of astrology a new, different and much simpler approach to his work with natal charts - bearing in mind the fact that he learns faster when he studies his own natal chart as he goes along, by applying to it what he has learned example-by-example herein.

Part One is augmented by the addition of some of my previously-published articles revised to some extent for inclusion here, which were not readily available to the average student otherwise. My indebtedness to the American Federation of Astrologers and others is appreciatively acknowledged in this connection.

Part Two

The last part of the book is devoted to an entirely original branch of the art arrived-at by this writer through diligent and extended research covering many authentic cases, and well provided with proven rules by which the student learns to tell the nature of an event that has already taken place but without being told anything in advance about what really happened.

This is but one of many methods definitely attesting to the value of astrology in our lives: it is unique in that it silences those who may question that fact though we astrologers know that the science needs no apology: and is further unique in that the rules are in great part equally applicable to natal charts.

Ivy M. Goldstein-Jacobson

MY NOTEBOOK FOR THE SUN

The Sun in your chart represents what you are all your life insofar as your individuality is concerned apart from your personality represented by the Moon, and your temperament, represented by the Ascendant & its ruler.   As he progresses through the Signs, he "naturalizes" you in them - much as regular naturalization in another country might do, where something new is added & nothing old taken away. The original stamp remains although it develops and rounds out as time goes on and experience leaves its mark on you.

The house your Sun is in at birth discloses where you shine best, the department your ego requires for self-expression, the best field of endeavor for your success. The Sign the Sun is in is the channel that he chooses to work through in that department and it makes a great difference whether that Sign is earth, fire, air or water in the development of your individuality, although we must always remember that they are all equally good and the Sun can shine anywhere.

Whether the Sign is cardinal, fixed or mutable at birth also shows its effect in the individuality the Sun discloses: the first forging ahead on its own, & the second plodding ahead to develop itself -- while the third is greatly affected by outside influences, thus able to adapt or adopt whatever is available to his use or purpose under the existing circumstances.

In angular houses (1st, 4th, 7th & 10th), the Sun makes your individuality more apparent to others and brings you into the limelight through your personal appeal; gives you an audience & some form of career having to do with management, association with those having a professional or other title, or with people

of distinction.   Your family considers you an asset
in some special way as an individual; children have
a place in your life & marriage brings ease or gain.
Whether or not you really possess great gifts of individuality or fitness to office, you will be given
higher position & greater appreciation when angular.

In succeedent houses (2nd, 5th, 8th and 11th) the
Sun reduces the amount of publicity you get based on
merits of individuality alone. Many with the Sun in
succeedent or cadent houses receive great publicity,
but not because of personal appeal: perhaps politics
or services of some kind bring us to public notice &
even acclaim, outside of any public awareness of our
inner individualism. Medicine, banking, handling of
other people's holdings or possessions, legislation,
the arts or research in scientific fields may do it.

In cadent houses (3rd, 6th, 9th and 12th) the Sun
shines best behind the scenes, so to speak, because
the individuality is expressed in fields of service,
whether that be in labor, teaching or writing, with
the unfortunate or downtrodden, in institutional departments, the church, and so on. The individuality
is more apparent to those in closer contact, arm-in-
arm as it were, and develops through misfortune in a
way, differing from the Sun in angular houses where
contact with other people is rather detached: there
they lend you a hand, but here you lend them a hand.

In an intercepted Sign at birth, the Sun is under
restraint in that department (house) in early life &
makes better progress as he gets out of the Sign and
thus out of bondage. More preparation for life is
required if the Sun is held in interception-abeyance
so that others are aware of the absence of something
essential toward his greater success. This may mean
lack of advantages, of opportunity, or of ambition.

Though an intercepted Sign widens the house it is in, enlarging the department, we note that the house remains quiescent if no planet is there, but if the progressing Sun enters the intercepted Sign it means that the native has deliberately sought retirement & privacy for activity aimed at advancement that is in some way allied to developing himself in some larger field. It is quite different from having the Sun in an intercepted Sign at birth, being intentional now. This intent on retirement for reasons of advancement is also shown by the Sun progressing into the 12th.

If the Sun is in mutual reception with the Moon or a planet (each in the other's natural Sign) it gives exchange status so that the Sun is enabled to follow two interests, or to change to another department if he so desires, and especially in order to get around difficulties or out of interception interfering with his progress as a person in his own right. Changes in the life occur thereby & usually for the better.

In passing, we may note that ANY planet in mutual reception brings changes for the better in the life.

In Fire Signs the Sun is naturally enthusiastic & quick in developing himself as an individual, brooking no interference; and earlier in Aries, generally with but little help; later in Leo, but with outside assistance; taking his time in Sagittarius, usually, until there is little left, yet he seems to need but little self-application after all, because he may be an "older soul" adequately developed for his chart.

In Earth Signs the Sun develops the individuality patiently, in an unhurried, determined way; persistently in Capricorn, stubbornly in Taurus, & cleverly in Virgo, but always with a fine sense of values and the capacity to wait & waste no scrap of experience.

In Air Signs, the Sun develops the individuality through logic, reason and keen insight into basic or underlying principles. It is therefore the most impersonal approach to the most personal development. In Libra, judiciously and calmly, sure of the laws & regulations he leans upon; in Gemini, with an open & inquiring mind, probing for what is factual; and in Aquarius, by depending on universal principles that he knows can ultimately be proven scientifically: an individuality at once remarkably human and godlike.

In Water Signs the Sun brings the subconscious to individual development of the ego-psyche, thus going deeper than in the other elements in his search for understanding which is always based on some form of faith that the native accepts proved or unproved. In Cancer, it is intuition; in Scorpio, investigation; in Pisces, psychic revelation. In all these, there is shared the power of extra-sensory perception that makes it natural to recognize spiritual truth as it unfolds, becoming a part of the ego & individuality.

Apply these keywords to your natal Sun to see the attributes of individuality you were born with -- as revealed by the Sign he was in at birth -- and then "naturalize" him with the additional attributes that he gained in progressing through additional Signs in developing your individuality and shaping it as your chart promised. Now you know where you stand today.

* * * * *

MY NOTEBOOK FOR THE MOON

Perhaps the best descriptive word we have for the Moon is CHANGE, and the house she appears in in your chart shows the department where you are most likely to experience the greatest changes in your life; and especially those that affect your future because the Moon is the developing-power and she ranges over the entire chart more than once in your lifetime, therefore the changes she initiates are very far-reaching in scope and will encompass your entire future.   If this were not so, life would be exceedingly humdrum.

As all changes in the life call for readjustment, those that are made under the conjunction, square or opposition cause drastic reactions, and particularly where malefics are involved (the more so if they are in angular houses, conferring more surety & strength and giving them "happenstance" or accidental power). The semisquare involves loss of friendships, money & possessions, because it is the natural distance from the Ascendant to the middle of the 11th & 2d Houses. The sesquare involves loss related to matters of the 5th & 9th Houses, being their midpoint distance from the Ascendant.   The quincunx measures to the cusps of the 6th & 8th Houses, forcing support of another, payment of his debts & funeral expenses, and so on.

The sextile, semisextile and trine give fortunate results in making changes - any upheaval is lessened in impact or is made pleasantly & easily or subtly.

As the Moon travels around the chart two or three times in the average life span, arousing each planet over and over again under diversified aspects, she registers your changes and their dates.   The more outstanding developments are those involving planets

she most strongly aspected at birth - giving preference to those that are angular, which is a clue that
helps you to evaluate the importance of the change.
Besides the regular Secondary Method of progression
(so many days after birth in the natal ephemeris for
so many years after birth) be sure to use the Direc-
tional Method, adding your age-in-years to the natal
planets and particularly to the Moon.   In this way,
additional changes are disclosed by her new aspects.

Your individual approach to each change is always
the same & is a subtle thing, more easily recognized
if you look back to the planet she last passed over
before your birth. She "picked up" something of its
nature, made it part of herself, & thereby developed
it as her finishing touch in your personality & temperament.   Both your Moon and you will express that
planet's nature in making & meeting changes in life.

If she last passed over Mars before your birth, a
spirit of daring and enterprise urges changes, which
are made on impulse and generally by taking chances,
preceded by great restlessness.   The goal is always
self-justification so that arguments usually follow.
Mars strikes, goes on strike, strikes back, & always
strikes out for himself.   He initiates bold changes
of his own volition. Look for these revealing characteristics in anyone whose Moon was last over Mars.

If Uranus, changes occur in your life suddenly or
unexpectedly and are usually very disruptive because
made under compulsion or force of circumstances. He
breaks away, breaks ties, and breaks up the existing
foundation at the time.   Freedom from domination is
the goal and you awake to its desirability.   Thence-
forward you operate under a new concept, with a certain genius for getting around difficulties, finding
the best solution each time or the quickest way out.

If last over the Sun before birth, the Moon shows changes that are well-timed & well-executed with the help of a superior but with the possibility of unintentional cruelty to someone, because she has picked up that imperialistic characteristic where "the king can do no wrong" even when he does: she has obtained conferred authority to act.   The goal is success at any cost and irresponsibility toward that cost, with others aware of the selfishness yet without rancor.

If Saturn, changes are planned ahead with shrewdness, no nonsense & no undue sentimentality. Timing is of the essence, and patience is part of it -- you know when and where to strike. Matters long pending precede the change, the solution is sensible & practicable, and any breaks are mended so that no actual definite break can operate: some attachment remains, because Saturn always keeps a string attached, never lets go entirely, and even retains his hold on the very minerals in your bones, which he governs, long after you have finished with them. Such changes are the most sensible of all because Saturn calculates.

If Neptune, there is secrecy or subterfuge, & the changes are dreamed-of, schemed-for & achieved with no full reason ever being given. The goal is Utopian and idealistic, naive & out-of-reach in some particular, preceded by bewilderment and followed later on by some evidence of self-defrauding, with remorse or regret long remembered. Someone or something is put aside, surrendered, alienated & rendered ineffectual forever. This type of change is the saddest of all.

If Mercury, there is cleverness in meeting or effecting changes in life though you may be too easily persuaded of their necessity, thus subject to error. Most of the changes under Mercury's subtle influence are preceded by much coming-&-going, correspondence,

discussion, dealings with agents, go-betweens, those
in the family or close to you; and generally involve
a document, ticket or signature and some annoyances.
Any decision is open to revision and readjustment as
well as re-hashing in the future.   Such changes are
susceptible to error, to explanation and correction.

If Jupiter, changes are made in the optimistic
hope that circumstances or a lucky break will do the
best for you; there is a certain flourish to the try
and almost always profit and a move higher up, such
as a promotion or other rise in life, because of the
ever-preceding faith and trust in the Almighty.   His
is the luckiest influence to be born under, all else
being equal, with most changes made for the better.

If Venus, the changes in your life are effected
smoothly and with intent to deal fairly even though
drastic in type, such as a divorce achieved amicably
without injustice to either party, preceded by quiet
and co-operative judgment. Harmony is your goal but
if the Moon's aspect to Venus was bad at birth there
is an urge to settle for peace at any price, which
may come high in the long run.   However, you remain
indulgent & forgiving, ever counting your blessings.

If Pluto, changes are made in silence, with some
withdrawal evident from then on. A group may be involved and an important person missing. There was a
preceding confused period in the life and the future
is always complicated somehow, because of readjust-
ments following more or less frequently in the wake
of a change Pluto influences; he compounds trouble.

Some changes involve reaching a critical stage so
that a simple adaptation is unattainable. This will
be the case if the natal Moon is in a "critical degree" (0, 13, 26 of cardinal Signs; 9, 21 of fixed,

4 and 17 of common Signs) denoting developments that
bring matters of the house to a crisis or climax de-
manding a different arrangement. This may or may not
be inharmoniously accomplished for good: sometimes a
crisis marks a turn for the better, even if severity
is required to bring matters to a head. The inflammatory planet Mars is sure to do this if your natal
Moon is in any aspect at all to him, but if she last
passed over him in your chart and is also in a critical degree there will be times in life when you may
say "Enough's enough!" and, precipitating a crisis,
cut the Gordian knot yourself for a personal change.

You must take three clues into consideration when
reading for the changes in your life - the nature of
the planet the Moon last passed over, the nature of
the aspect they made and whether or not she is in a
critical degree. Last over any planet and in a bad
aspect to it signifies that you follow that planet's
nature but take drastic steps in making changes, and
if the Moon is in a critical degree there will be an
unavoidable crisis to handle. This is forewarning.

Besides the critical degrees we are reminded that
if the natal Moon is in the 29th degree of any Sign
(and especially Taurus, the place of the Pleiades or
so-called Weeping Sisters) it is considered ominous
in the matters of the house she occupies, and there
will be something to weep about in making important
changes there. Even when the natal Moon is not thus
ill-starred, if any planet or cusp is in 29 degrees
at birth the Moon will progress to aspect it & cause
a disturbance which upsets the status quo there, and
especially if any change is under way at the time.

The Sun, Moon or any planet in plus-0 degrees at
birth has its Solstice Point (see p. 103) in 29 degrees of another Sign, marking that a disappointment

area when activated by the progressed Moon's square, because she will be afflicting that point and changing Signs also, signifying a very upsetting change.

The Moon increasing in light at your birth (going away from the Sun) emphasizes the effects of changes in your life so that they get larger, looming up importantly in the future, thereby remembered. If she is decreasing in light at your birth (moving toward the Sun) whatever was an early afflictive-change in your life will peter out in importance to you, & you "get over it" in time, without anger or retaliation.

If your natal Moon is in a Sign following the one holding the Sun, we see that your mother deferred to your father's wishes and followed his lead as a matter of policy: but if she is in a Sign preceding the one holding the Sun, your mother led the way for him and all changes were made according to her decision.

If your natal Moon last passed over a malefic before your birth no matter how far back in the chart, your mother suffered an accident or some disability during the prenatal period which affected your body, changing its appearance, form or functional capacity to some extent - and usually in the part of the body that is ruled by the Sign occupied by that malefic.

If the natal Moon is besieged in your chart (that is, between two malefics no matter how far apart) it signifies that one unhappy change leads to another. If last over a malefic and next over a benefic, previous unhappy changes are not likely to be repeated: we count the Sun & Mercury as benefics in such cases unless square the Ascendant. If last over a benefic and next over a malefic, a gainful change will still have some repercussions that cause disparagement or frustration in the future. If between benefics, the

Moon makes good moves followed by other good moves:
one gainful change leads to another gainful change.

If your natal Moon is in mutual reception in your
chart (such as the Moon in Libra & Venus in Cancer),
it denotes that whatever changes are entered into by
mutual consent with another person can be gotten out
of in the same way, since they have exchange status.

The Moon above the horizon at birth operates more
openly in formulating a change than when below the
horizon at birth: still more apparent when she is in
an angular house. On the oriental side of the chart
(the Ascendant side) her most outstanding change related to the house she is in occurs earlier in life
than when she is on the occidental side of the chart
(the Descendant side), when you are past your youth.

The 8th, 12th and 4th Houses are unfortunate on
their own account (death, misfortune and the grave),
the 5th and 9th in the way they could turn out, because their end-of-the-matter-4th Houses are the 8th
and 12th. We ourselves may be considered to be born
handicapped by the sins of our fathers since our own
1st House (the body: the matter we are made of), has
as its end-of-that-matter house the 4th itself, ruling both the father and the grave: a grave matter to
be born of a human father at all, so to speak. The
Moon in any of these houses denotes changes accounting for many of our ill-advised & unfortunate moves.

The Moon in angular houses (1st, 4th, 7th & 10th)
signifies changes that bring publicity, presence in
court, relinquishment of real estate, wide dispersal
of the family, some domestic discord, changes in the
home and in the place of employment, and sometimes a
change in previously-settled funeral arrangements,
made for or by the person whose horoscope it is.

DELINEATION OF THE NATAL MOON

5:23:19 a.m. LMT June 19, 1896 - 39N16 76W41
(The Duchess of Windsor)

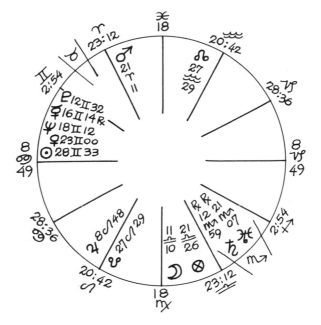

A medium tall woman of great charm and sincerity, slender, dark hair and eyes, of faultless taste, and wearing her clothes with distinction. Many changes and misfortunes in early childhood, death of father; several divorces; no children; attainment of wealth.

The Moon in succeedent houses (2nd, 5th, 8th and
11th) is more retiring by nature, and her changes do
not come to public attention but do leave their mark
forever on the private life. Sometimes the position
in life changes because of the death of a relative.
Circumstances undergo many ups & downs: friendships,
lovers, even children change: usually the parents do
not provide adequately for the native's future which
is ruled by the 2nd House and subject to opposition,
square or conjunction by the Moon when succeedent.

The Moon in cadent houses (3rd, 6th, 9th & 12th)
makes changes not to the native's best interests and
commits him to a disadvantage that he may not recognize until too late. Any publicity is not of his
seeking. His education is lacking in some important
"finish" and his religious beliefs or observances do
not follow his family's: he is a changeling there in
some way. He leaves his place of birth, changes address frequently, usually has less to do with family
members than otherwise or remains in the background;
and in later life he worries about changes in health
or appearance.   He will not land where he planned.

In the chart opposite, the Moon in the 4th will
upset family continuity, domestic harmony, continued
residence at the same address, & even funeral plans.
The relatives are dispersed, and the Duchess experiences changes that bring publicity, legal actions or
presence in court, & ownership of land late in life.
Last over Jupiter, changes are made for the better &
involve a rise in life.   Her outstanding change was
her marriage to the abdicated King of England bringing her a promotion of sorts accompanied by a title,
great wealth and ownership of much property of value
both real and personal.   Everything would naturally
increase for her, with her Moon increasing in light,
last over Jupiter and sextile Jupiter-of-increase.

★ ★ ★ ★ ★

Planets in Mutual Reception

Two rulers in each other's Sign always see
eye to eye. It means they share and share alike,
so nothing goes awry. And even if they break a rule
or some convention flout --- whatever one gets into,
the other gets him out.

Neptune in the 7th House

With Neptune in your 7th House
    You idolize your mate.
You do not meet by happenstance,
    You always meet by Fate.
You do not stop to understand
    Or marvel how it feels:
The moment that you take her hand
    You fall head over heels.

Both Rulers Retrograde

They married for companionship
    Drawn by the human flame,
But nothing came of it at all
    And life went on the same.

The magic words of love they sought
    And the romantic rapture
Were fantasies that went unwrought,
    And dreams too shy to capture.

But that was very long ago -
    They saw it through somehow;
Never to know what made it so -
    Unless they know it now?

* * * * *

MY NOTEBOOK FOR SATURN

Saturn is the Taskmaster, the Greater Malefic and finally the Reaper in life, exacting responsibility, inflicting denial & punishment and in the end Death. Yet he is probably our greatest friend because it is only through his lessons that we improve as humans & learn the humility entitling us to pass the Portals. His injury is permanent, but so is his great reward.

1.   The house in which Saturn appears in your natal chart is the 6th House of another house there, which represents a person for whom you take on some kind of work or whose responsibilities you assume. He is difficult to get along with, and he suffers from an illness that becomes chronic toward the end of life.

2.   Saturn below the horizon denotes one who prizes his privacy and likes to enclose his property with a fence, preferring seclusion and usually desirous of living alone in the latter years of his life.

3.   Where you find Saturn by house you locate someone of that house who wastes your time and holds you back from your preferred work, deliberately or not.

4.   A good aspect between your natal Saturn & Mars shows that you leave something of value to posterity including a house that you will build for yourself.

5.   The degree in which the natal Saturn appears is often indicative of the native's age at a future important event, but if he is retrograde there will be a delaying action. If he is in a cadent house, the main circumstance related to the event is delayed in coming to his attention, sometimes involving years.

6.   If Saturn is in a cadent house at birth he will
hold up matters of the house for later development &
if retrograde he will delay them unduly or deny them
altogether. He brings secret worry about the health
in later life and some chronic affliction.   In evil
aspect to Mercury, injury by scurrilous reports. Ir
any aspect to Mars, a relative suffers fatal injury.

7.   The first angular house Saturn enters following
birth or is already in at birth sets the pattern you
will adhere to in life, always related to the nature
of that house.   We use the transiting Saturn after
birth in this connection (and note that he may enter
the house by either direct or retrograde motion).

8.   When the natal Saturn is between two malefics,
no matter how far away they may be or whether or not
they are in aspect with him, the father suffers some
misfortune affecting the native's future and the two
may not agree - in fact, they may actively disagree.

9.   Saturn afflicting the natal Ascendant or in any
angular house and thereby afflicting the First House
causes much dentistry.   In a horary chart, it shows
a querent having bad teeth now or recent dentistry.

10.   If your natal Saturn is retrograde you are held
back from full enjoyment of whatever is mainly ruled
by the house he is in; and whatever benefit you gain
there comes later in life after you have earned it.
A planet retrograde encourages the native & the person of the house the planet is in to go back and try
again, thus Saturn retrograde allows reconciliation.

11.   If natal Saturn is in the Sign on the next-fol-
lowing house it shows disappointment in the matters
ruled by that next house, since he is connected with
it by the 12th-House (disappointment) relationship.

12.   If the natal Saturn is in mutual reception with another planet (each in the other's natural Sign) it denotes that they have exchange status so that they may be read, also, as though back in their own Signs still carrying the same degree: show Saturn's symbol where it would thus appear in his own Sign, and give him a secondary reading in that new house. It shows where the native may do equally well if he wishes to change places or take on an additional kind of work.

13.   Wherever you have Saturn by house, that is the department where you "take over the management" of its affairs (and sometimes of its persons, as well).

14.   Saturn conjunct or opposition the Sun or Moon, and any of them also in bad aspect to the Ascelli in 6 Leo or Antares in 8 Sagittarius denotes weak eyes, and sometimes a noticeable difference in their color or setting.   Cataracts are included in the same effects if the Pleiades in 29 Taurus are in the same relationship - and if it is Caput Algol in 24 Taurus the effect on the eyesight itself is very serious.

15.   Saturn in a Critical Degree (see p. 10) brings matters of the house he is in to a critical stage or crisis whenever he is afflicted by bad aspect from a progressed planet or major transit, as an eclipse.

16.   Saturn and Venus in opposition cools the affectional nature, bringing common sense into affairs of the heart. It also denotes rejection of the native (or querent in a horary chart) by someone of importance, usually a parent because these two planets are secondary significators of the father and mother.

17.   Saturn the thrifty in the same Sign with Jupiter the extravagant denotes a penny-wise-&-pound-foolish tendency in the native, the querent, or Government.

18. When the declination of natal Saturn is within
orb of parallel to that of any other planet, Sun and
Moon included, he has a steadying influence on that
other, making it steadfast and faithful to a trust.
The person's character is crystallized into definite
lines in early childhood - and since the parallel is
similar to the conjunction, the characteristics of
each planet will be easily recognized in the person.

19. Saturn's Solstice Point is his distance from 0-
Cancer or 0-Capricorn, whichever is nearer, carried
over to the other side (see p. 103). This point receives aspects from progressed planets and angles &,
moving forward at the rate of a degree a year, makes
aspects to natal planets and angles. This indicates
Saturnian developments involving heavy work or much
responsibility, long waiting, colds, falls, disability, dentistry, deaths in the circle - and so forth.

20. When transiting Saturn is in an empty house in
the chart and therefore more or less inactive, watch
for any lunation that conjoins him. A matter of the
house or a person there will then become active in a
new development if it is a New Moon: if it is a Full
Moon something long-pending will work to completion.

21. When an eclipse falls on your Saturn, timing an
event, look forward in the current ephemeris for the
dates on which the Sun will square and oppose that
eclipse degree, because that is when there is likely
to be some repercussion & sometimes a related event.

22. Being a slow-moving planet and not forming many
aspects by Secondary progression, Saturn should also
use the degree-for-a-year rate when being progressed
either directly or conversely. This never fails to
produce a series of strong aspects with outstanding
impact in the life not revealed by Saturn otherwise.

23.   Saturn in Earth or Air Signs at birth possesses
inner dignity and is better able to meet misfortune
& rudeness with equanimity.   Only Uranus who strikes
unseen with unpredictable and irresistible force can
find Saturn unprepared and thus vulnerable.   Always
expect disruptive events to occur when Saturn progresses to conjunct or afflict the natal Uranus and
rouse him into lightning retaliation - at which time
Saturn's equanimity and independence may desert him.

24.   Saturn in Gemini or aspecting planets in Gemini
has many dealings with relatives, neighbors & children. He shows much painstaking writing & re-writing
of the same thing & will repeat himself in speaking.

25.   Aspects to Saturn tell us by their nature how a
person will use the power Saturn gives simply by being aspected anywhere in the chart.   Squares galvanize us into making opportunities & trouble for ourselves; oppositions slow us down & we delay full use
of the power until late in life.   The quincunx makes
us reorganize our plans or eliminate non-essentials,
and something or somebody usually has to move out of
our way, giving us our desired opportunity at last.

26.   Any aspect between Saturn and another planet in
a natal chart joins their powers there & unites them
in the person whose chart it is, conferring upon him
their impersonal powers for his personal use, always
characterized by a tactful or cautious turn of mind.

27.   The year in which your Saturn changes direction
either direct or retrograde marks the passing of an
important older person in your life. Not only should
we note the number of days (called years) in which
this happens after birth, allowing ourselves 90 days
to denote 90 years of life, but also the same 90-day
period before birth denoting 90 years after birth.

28.   Saturn's distance from the Horizon carried over
to the other side, or from the Meridian carried over
to the other side, marks his Horizontal and Meridian
Parallel points.   Any other planet coming to such a
point forms a parallel to Saturn and promises an important Saturnian development in the person's life.

29.   Any angle coming to the midpoint between Saturn
and any other planet forms the Rapt Parallel between
the two, causing a noteworthy result at that time.

30.   Any affliction between Saturn and Mars (crisis)
brings old matters to a head or climax.   This is not
always without benefit to the native or querent, who
may profit thereby - the more so if either planet is
well-aspected to the Ascendant or to a planet there.

31.   Saturn in the 1st House or the 1st Quadrant at
birth throws burdens on the native early in life and
usually traceable to the father's misfortunes.   This
also denotes a certain self-consciousness of manner.

32.   Saturn in the 2nd or 8th House at birth denotes
power to save money, and a tendency to hoard various
amounts in easily accessible but different places.
If the natal or horary Saturn is in the 2nd House, &
the Sun rules or is in the 11th House (great expectations) watch for the date when the Sun conjoins him
either by regular progression or horary transit, because that is the time he brings you something old
or used or dark in color which you have long wanted.

33.   Saturn in the 3rd or 4th builds up an estate of
value; if retrograde, it comes later in life. In the
3rd it also points to a relative who withholds for
a time at least something that is rightfully yours.
When in the 3rd House Saturn causes tardy receipt of
news and notifications, also of important documents.

34.   Saturn in the 4th denotes a cramped grave and a
plain tombstone in an older, smaller burial ground.
The home is also dark, cold, gloomy & uncomfortable.

Saturn in the 4th House or first entering it by
transit into an angular house after birth signifies
inheritance in due course & ownership of real estate
in due time, often coming from the person he rules.

35.   Saturn in the 5th House gives grasping children
and responsibility because of them: joint ownership,
community property holdings and speculation threaten
to turn out at a loss: a very poor or stingy parent.

36.   Saturn in the 6th House takes on much hard work
voluntarily and with little profit or appreciation.
If afflicted he denotes danger from vicious animals.

37.   Saturn in the 7th House or first entering it by
transit into an angular house after birth signifies
marriage in due course but death of the partner.   If
he rules or is in the 7th House of any chart (natal,
mundane or horary) look for the mistake in figuring
or entering the symbols that will surely be present.

38.   Saturn in the 8th House promises gain by "goods
of the dead" and through wills, legacies and settlements or time payments such as alimony.   He denotes
shrewdness in managing other people's money & goods.
Death comes late in life to the native or querent.

39.   Saturn in the 9th House reveals that any second
marriage will involve an appreciable time-difference
either in ages or the event itself.   In any cadent
house Saturn has a leaning toward religion, the more
likely to be actively followed when in the 9th.   He
denotes serious illness of a family member, and some
caretaking required of the person whose chart it is.

40. Saturn in the 10th House shows many a fall both
physical and circumstantial.   Afflicted, he injures
the credit and reputation.   In mundane charts & certain horary questions he denotes death by execution;
also, the disgrace of rulers & government officials.
The 10th cusp progressing to conjunct Saturn in this
house or the 11th signifies a death in the family.

41. Saturn in the 11th House, being eight after the
4th and representing the department of deaths in the
family, signifies that the native will outlive many
in the family. However, this is not a good position
for great expectations, continued friendships & memberships or fulfillment of hopes and wishes: circumstances in general suffer, more especially when Saturn is afflicted by progressions or major transits.

42. Saturn (also Mars and Uranus) in your 12th signifies alienation from your father, and you may not
attend his funeral.   If afflicted, the native makes
many mistakes and false moves, and is also in danger
at the hands of an older person behind the scenes.

       If Saturn rules the 12th cusp and is angular at
birth, he warns that the skeleton in the closet will
surely come out into the open.   The secret & private
affairs will be made public, causing embarrassment.

43. If Saturn rules the 8th cusp, the Part of Peril
will exactly conjunct the Ascendant (see p. 150) and
if afflicted at birth will make the native accident-
prone (see page 77).   Saturn is the Greater Malefic
and his injury is always permanent, but if in mutual
reception he allows the native or querent to get out
of the worst of whatever he gets into, except death.

                    ✺ ✺ ✺ ✺ ✺

MY NOTEBOOK FOR MARS

Where Saturn may be said to cut DOWN and Uranus to cut THROUGH, Mars is the one who cuts OUT. He is the surgeon or butcher, or the efficiency expert, as the case may be. In any aspect to the Moon at birth they function according to this differentiation, and particularly as regards the matters and people ruled by the houses they occupy. In proceedings involving red tape or observance of formal rules & regulations Saturn reduces the amount, Uranus ignores it (substituting a newer short-cut method of his own devising) but Mars handles it by disposing of it entirely and ending up without it - as in surgery, a more or less violent cutting-out measure. Where we find Mars we always find developments requiring drastic action but always the ability to dispose of them forever. It is his "I can do without it if I must" attitude.

In reading an aspect between natal planets, always name the faster planet first. Thus, Mars may apply to or separate from an aspect of Jupiter, Saturn, Uranus, Neptune & Pluto because he moves faster than they. But being slower than the Moon, Mercury, Venus and the Sun, we always name them first so that they apply to or separate from an aspect to him. By this we recognize that some relationship is either going to develop between them or has already done so.

1.   Where your Mars is based at birth shows what is "cut out to be cut out" in your life: the condition, person or thing that you will have to go on without.

2.   If your Mars is applying to an aspect at birth, you make every effort to build into your consciousness whatever the other one has to give, because you are looking toward that other for it: his separating

aspects disclose what you have already acquired from that other planet's best attributes and now express.

3.   If your natal Mars makes no applying aspect at all, you are an unusually independent, self-reliant and self-sufficient person who never looks to anyone else for aid, protection or encouragement, & you are violently averse to being led, directed or dictated-to by others, because you know you are possessed of adequate power to handle any contingency unassisted.

4.   If another planet is applying to Mars at birth, someone else comes to you for aid or encouragement: but if another planet is separating from an aspect to Mars it is a denial of further familiarity, since the other has accepted what he wanted and has gone on his way, better armed than he was.   Even if the other retrogrades back to aspect Mars again, he only returns for more of the same for himself because his original relationship stamped him for all time as a taker with Mars the giver, and it will be again followed by a continuing denial of further familiarity.

5.   When Mars and another planet are conjunct or in parallel of declination only, we disregard the applying-or-separating principle and read them as joining their attributes mutually in you from birth, and you possess their co-operative, interchangeable benefit. Saturn and Mars together are like two people walking arm-in-arm: the plodder quickens his pace, the racer slows down: each has consideration for the other and that is a quality you thereby possess and express.

6.   Mars in good aspect to Saturn is more likely to look before he leaps, to count the cost and plan his next move and see it accomplished, but in bad aspect it is just the reverse.   If they are trine, you are a hard worker and may have a capital M in your name.

7.   Any aspect between Mars & the Sun or Moon will strengthen the body & its capacity to function but a bad aspect (with either luminary conjunct or opposition a malefic fixed star (see page 19) weakens the eyes. In a horary chart it denotes great eyestrain.

8.   Any aspect between the Moon & Mars at birth is indicative of surgery, either major or minor but not necessarily fatal. Operations are usually timed in such cases by major progressions combined with heavy transits & aspect the Ascendant to make it physical.

9.   In practically any aspect to Jupiter or Venus, Mars is luckier than he realizes, if we take his bad aspects elsewhere into consideration. The benefics pull the punches of those bad aspects: they slap you for your own good: you are less brash & extravagant.

10. Mars and Neptune in aspect give love of color & ability to use it to advantage: it also gives a more colorful life, but under bad aspects there is danger of being defrauded & fooled where Neptune is housed.

11. Mars at birth squared by the Moon in the 8th accounts for the early death of the mother in childbirth, but this rule fails without at least two more dire indications of the same calamity to confirm it.

12. If Mars is the planet the Moon first conjuncts or opposes after birth, it signifies difficulties in marriage: separation, divorce or widowhood probable.

13. Mars and Mercury in aspect give eloquence with words, especially in debates, also with gestures and expressions that convey a meaning (waving, nodding, winking, smiling, grimacing, etc.) and facility with instruments or machines used in writing; also with things signalling a message, such as flags & flares.

14. Mars in the exact degree held by the nodes (and
whether it is a good or bad aspect) points to a person represented by the house Mars is in who suffers
some casualty or other misfortune in his life that
requires your assistance or sympathetic attention.

15. Mars quincunx any planet (one side or the other
of being in opposition) puts forth a worthy effort
for an unworthy cause in assisting a non-cooperative
person represented by that planet in that house, because it is love's labor lost. You may have to support him, pay his debts or put up bail for him, because Mars is approachable in troubled times. Also,
he reorganizes matters of the house the planet is in
by labor or by dispensing with non-essentials there.

16. Mars besieged (between malefics, no matter how
far apart & whether or not they are in aspect) puts
you on the horns of a dilemma at some time, when you
will have to cut your way out by very drastic means.

17. The people you have dealings with through planets in aspect with Mars are personified by the planets plus the houses they are in.   For instance, the
Moon or Venus in the 6th House describes a woman and
presumably an aunt, employe, co-worker, healer, tenant or other 6th-House female; whereas the remaining
planets there, being masculine, personify a male co-
worker, an uncle, and so forth.   The aspect itself
discloses whether or not such dealings are pleasant.

18. Bear with the one who is rude to you, knowing
that he is struggling to overcome his own Mars which
must be square to a malefic planet in his own chart.

19. Your Mars in a Mercury-ruled Sign (Gemini, Virgo) or in the Mercury decanate of any Air or Earth
Sign, or in mutual reception with Mercury, believes

that his pen is mightier than his sword. He is very
persuasive either in Mercury-logic or Mars-argument.

20. Your Mars in a Venus-ruled Sign (Taurus, Libra)
or in the Venus decanate of any Earth or Air Sign or
in mutual reception with Venus at birth, discloses
that you are much kinder and gentler than you seem,
susceptible to persuasion, desirous of appreciation,
perhaps envious of beauty, very interested in marriage and attractive to the opposite sex, and given to
hiding your iron hand in a velvet glove on occasion.

21. Mars in the first half of a Sign expresses more
on the mental side and in a leading capacity because
that is the "head" part of the Sign. The last half
is the "feet" part of the Sign, where Mars expresses
more on the physical side & in a following capacity.

22. Mars by Sign tells the part of the body liable
to inflammatory pathology, and in the first decanate
it is in the upper part of the organ. In the second
decanate, the middle part; and in the last decanate,
it is the lower part of the organ. He is most harm-
ful in his debility-Signs, Libra, Taurus and Cancer.

23. When Mars at birth is in a Critical Degree (0,
13, 26 of cardinal Signs; 9, 21 of fixed Signs; 4, 17
of common Signs), matters where he is based at birth
will reach a critical stage or crisis requiring cutting loose forever from the situation there & severing bonds or ties. This results in alienation and
estrangement that endures, and is much more damaging
than the crisis Mars develops in any house simply by
being there, whether or not critical or afflicted.

24. Where your Mars is by house, there do you know
someone who possesses a weapon or means of doing you
harm, and if in bad aspect with the Ascendant he may

use that weapon or power against you or threaten to. But if Mars is in mutual reception anywhere in your chart no harm can touch you because it is deflected.

25. If natal Mars is retrograde it denotes power to go back and try again, to reconcile differences with others, and to wage a winning fight within yourself.

26. Mars' latitude seems to be greatest around 4:15 degrees.   The closer your Mars' latitude comes to this tells how much latitude YOU take in expressing his traits, and how much scope you allow yourself in ventures & adventures, and how angry you can become.

27. When progressed or prenatal Mars changes direction, either retrograde or direct, he times a death in your circle and a decided change in your affairs.

28. Besides progressing Mars by the usual Secondary Method (a DAY for a year in the natal ephemeris) the Solar Arc Method of a DEGREE for a year should also be used, to know the additional periods of life when Mars will be active. By subtracting the arc instead of adding it, the converse-Mars position is located. His converse conjunctions are generally destructive.

29. In either 0-degrees or 29-degrees at birth Mars has to do with events that occur before the first birthday, because 0-degrees denotes months of life & the 29th degree has 0-degrees as its Solstice Point. The 29th degree is ominous in action when stimulated by progressions or heavy transits. It also includes age 29 for an overt & ill-advised undertaking. When your progressed or Solar-directed Mars reaches 29 of any Sign, aspected or not, you will act too hastily.

30. Mars is one of the restless planets (with Uranus, Mercury & the Moon), seldom at home when angular

or cadent, and more content to be domestic when in a succeedent house. He "stays put" longest when in a fixed Sign, and does not give up or give in easily.

31. You can generally have what you want from the house Mars is in at birth, depending on how much of an effort you will make in your own behalf. If you are willing to battle for it you can win. You stand the best chance if Mars is in the 11th House because that department has a blanket coverage on all your hopes and wishes, and Mars there can fight for them.

32. Mars angular brings trouble out into the open, but also the capacity to handle it. Difficulty at the time of birth but survival. Danger of violence to the body by blows, accidents or surgery. Clashes with the authorities over possibly-undeserved dis- credit: demand to see your credentials. Marriage is terminated by separation, divorce or widowhood. He times the death of a prominent member of the family.

33. Mars succeedent has less trouble that comes to light and is more independent of circumstances, pos- sessions and people: he can take them or leave them with equal equanimity but holds them best by loosing them and letting them go, as the Bible says to do. He gives freely, but not a necessary weapon or tool.

34. Mars in a cadent house causes much trouble be- hind the scenes and probability of airing it in the newspapers. Difficulty at home, in school, and with strangers. Digestive disturbances & possibility of abdominal operations, with reaction to vaccination & inoculation, etc. He shows procrastination in some special instance causing loss of a good opportunity: the native or querent should therefore remember that "He who will not when he may, may not when he will."

35. Mars oriental (on the Ascendant side) is more
prone to accidents.   On the occidental (Descendant)
side of the chart Mars is more liable to illnesses.
In either case what you suffer borders on the acute.

36. In the First Quadrant (between the 1st and 4th
cusps) Mars is in danger of self-imposed accidents &
operations.   In horary, he says NO to the question,
and discloses trouble coming up -- sooner if direct.

37. Mars in the First House or above the horizon is
more likely to make his own way in life, and has the
energy & stamina and also the opportunity to do it.
Mars there always takes the line of most resistance.
In the First House (Present) Mars lives hard & fast.

38. Mars below the horizon & not in the First House
takes the line of least resistance and requires outside contribution to his progress or to his program.

39. Mars in the Second House (your Future) denotes
trouble coming up in your life and in a horary question - but not as immediately as in the First House.
If retrograde, he signifies extravagance & damage to
possessions, & a known ancestor who died in battle.

40. Mars in the Third House brings attempted attack
behind the scenes of the home, which may be physical
or scandalous as directed against the person through
his family, and if afflicting the Ascendant there is
some degree of harm to the native or to the querent.

41. Mars in the Fourth House, especially afflicted,
may "burn the house down or burn the family up". He
sometimes describes a father who attempts suicide.
If natal Mars is retrograde in the 4th House and remains so throughout life, final burial does not take
place until he changes to direct, thus signifying a

change of resting-place having to do with the grave,
which is ruled by the 4th House.   Consult the natal
ephemeris for the progressed year of his turning.   A
woman will be older at marriage than her mother was.

42.   Mars in or ruling the 5th in a woman's chart &
conjunct or in bad aspect to Neptune threatens abor-
tions or miscarriages.   Children will lack ambition.
Danger of injury or accidents at pleasure resorts.

43.   Mars in the 6th House and near the 7th cusp can
annul marriage and break contracts or leases through
craftiness.   If afflicted, danger from pet animals.
Acute illness running a high fever that is curative.
Mars six houses after one bearing his Sign Aries or
Scorpio upsets the routine or system where he rules,
& distresses the people represented there, according
to his actions (aspects) in the house he is in.   For
example: if he is afflicted in the 9th and rules the
4th, his absence from home & especially his tendency
to roam afar, his difficulties at college, disagree-
ment with religious tenets, arguments with strangers
and in-laws, failure to take out insurance, etc. may
upset domestic affairs & routine, distress the family
and cause loss of real estate & inheritance rights.

44.   Mars in the Seventh House denotes lawsuits, and
if afflicted or in Cancer it will be a lost cause or
a judgment that cannot be collected.   In a mundane
chart he signifies war brewing.   In a natal chart he
is always seven houses after another which rules the
person whose marital break-up may involve you.   Mars
in the 5th shows a friend's marital break-up and you
somewhere in the picture.   In the 9th, you are drawn
into a relative's or neighbor's divorce. In the 11th
you appear at the divorce hearing for your children.
In the 12th, you testify for a servant or relative &
in the 1st itself you testify at your own divorce.

45.   Mars in the Eighth House denotes major or minor
surgery: the mate possesses firearms: trouble in the
home of the married first child: a Will favors you.
Mars is always eight houses after one in the chart
whose persons or material possessions he takes away,
or at least out of your keeping. (See paragraph 48)

46.   Mars in the Ninth House meets danger far afield
or in foreign lands & may die there. (See para. 43)

47.   Mars in the Tenth House suffers undeserved discredit.   The person must learn to lower his voice.

48.   Mars in the 11th House is in the 8th department
of death for the family-4th, signifying many deaths
in the family (one by violence), so that you outlive
most of your family if not all. This house lies between the 10th-of-success and the 12th-of-failure so
that it rules your circumstances in general that may
take you up or down in life. Mars here denotes many
changes in your circumstances (because he is a restless planet) and the main changes are usually caused
by a death in the family.   This house is sextile to
the 1st House, so changing circumstances do no harm.

49.   Mars in the 12th House or 12th Sign Pisces, or
conjunct Neptune, brings tribulation in life and the
person may be unfortunate in some particular, or may
have to work alone or secluded to a great extent.
Mars is always twelve houses after one whose affairs
displease you & must be handled with more discretion
than otherwise.   Thus, in the First House there will
be need to husband the finances as ruled by the next
house - or in the Fourth House a child is unruly, or
joint holdings or community property is not secure.

☆ ☆ ☆ ☆ ☆

MY NOTEBOOK FOR MERCURY

The planet that rules our capacity to adapt ourselves mentally to conditions & situations is thereby our saving grace toward sanity and survival on
earth, and that planet is Mercury. His metal quick-
silver (or mercury) possesses the power of immediate
adaptation to persuasion since, unlike other metals,
it is fluid and free-moving, taking quickly & easily
any direction the exigencies of the moment require,
and that is how our mental awareness normally works.
In thought & speech he rules the subject under discussion: his is a subject metal and subjective mind.
Through him we have mental control that can heal us.

Mercury being dual responds twice to the pressure
a prevailing condition may exert on the person, such
as his first uneasy awareness of something wrong and
his second easy-or-uneasy awareness that something
must be done about it - and therein lies the enigma:
what does the chart show the person may do about it?

In your natal chart Mercury discloses your adapt-
ive equipment, your capacity to adjust to conditions
that beset you, your philosophical ability to accept
or escape from the overwhelming effects of grief and
worry, disappointment, remorse, loneliness, monotony
and frustration and bitter memory that may otherwise
take their toll of the health. These were not present at birth, but your natal Mercury reveals how you
will face them: whether you will be realistic and do
something or unrealistic and do nothing mentally, to
meet the trouble head-on and vanquish it. In a Sign
ruled by Mars, Saturn or Uranus, or in any aspect to
these planets, Mercury is quicker to take action and
do something in his own behalf although he may delay
in standing up for himself if Mercury is retrograde.

Mercury, whose symbol is the caduceus or wand of the physician, is the healing force that is resident in the mind and designed to control body functions. As natal Mercury goes, so goes your healing power.

Mercury is that Power that brings the Aries brain to life. The whole body is composed of individual cells, every one of them possessing intelligence for the necessary control to keep blood-cells and flesh-cells, bone-cells and hair-cells, etc. from marrying out of the religion, so to speak, which would result in anatomical chaos. Besides intelligence, however, to the brain-cells alone is vouchsafed intellect and inspiration, the avenue to divine understanding, and the only power we have to cure ourselves sans drugs. We can direct our intellect toward the intelligence of body-cells gone wrong and heal them by persuasion because intelligence is always subject to intellect. Other life-forms have instinct instead of intellect. A good clue to the person's capacity to heal himself or to cure himself of the wrong response to troubles may be found by studying Mercury in his natal chart, disclosing his way of taking flight from reality.

People are commonly classed as introverts or extroverts, the former inclined to turn & look inward, the latter looking outward. They get away from dissatisfaction by turning their individual way so that extroverts dispel their discontent by running away from it, as an unhappily-married person will turn to someONE else, an outer interest: whereas the unhappy introvert turns to someTHING else of inner interest: each takes flight from reality in his own way but it is the way his natal Mercury directs. Whether it is the best way is something the astrologer can reveal.

Extroverts generally have their planets dispersed around the wheel. When cornered by a question they can't or won't answer they spread out like their planets & talk in all directions or change the subject. Good politicians are notable for this: listen to them on the "Meet the Press" program and you will readily recognize the extroverts: they get outside a problem question and are very diffusive. Their Mercury is usually direct, at least in the adult years.

Introverts generally have their planets more concentrated in the chart. They stay on the beam as it were and go to great lengths to bring out the answer to a problem question (sometimes maddeningly so) and especially if their Moon has wide latitude (5:18 being the widest): they take in more territory then, & no smallest detail escapes them. Their Mercury is usually retrograde at birth, probing within for the answer to a question, mostly achieved by in-tuition.

Both these types think and talk equally well, but the extrovert ranges all over the field while the introvert confines himself to his thesis and stays with it to the end, coming back to it after any interruption, whereas the extrovert usually leaves it dangling in the stratosphere. We always know where we stand with the introvert because he never evades the issue. Thus the introvert is more realistic in facing facts and life - although it may be that the extrovert is thus freer and less frustrated in life.

Both are important and worthwhile individuals but they need to have their special aptitudes developed early in life with equal care, if they are to register in the world as adults with equal success. To do this, it is essential that we examine the chart carefully for the aptitudes shown by the aspects between Mercury and the other planets, & by the Sign & condition he is in. Mercury is good in any Sign but specifically so for the person whose chart it is.

1.   The house your Mercury is in at birth is the 3d
of decisions after another house which represents a
person for whom you will often make major decisions.

2.   Subtract the number of the house your Mercury
is in from 14: this gives the number of the house in
which your decisions or opinions register strongly.

3.   Where Saturn is a tool & Mars a weapon, Mercury
is an instrument, the keenest & most useful of all.
The fine arts, the liberal arts and the mechanical &
industrial arts all require Mercury but differently.
If in mutual reception, you possess more than one.

4.   Mercury in aspect with Mars will walk quickly &
speak rapidly and positively and debate every point.
Any aspect between them shows trouble with kinfolk.

5.   Mercury in good aspect to Saturn denotes a fine
memory. Usually the father is more friendly. A bad
aspect denotes absentmindedness; also, the father is
more distant in his manner, or often away from home.

6.   If your Mercury rises ahead of the Sun, logic &
reason guide you in life. If after the Sun, you are
led by spur-of-the-moment decisions made on impulse.

7.   Mercury in Fire & Air Signs has more healing or
curative powers by directing the mind exclusively at
the time toward the trouble or the place of illness.
Mercury in Gemini has healing in his hands & speech.

Mercury Retrograde

8.   People with Mercury retrograde are often very
shy.   They love the Sun but seek the shade, and let
the world go by.   It isn't that they are afraid --
it's only that they're shy.

✮ ✮ ✮ ✮ ✮

MY NOTEBOOK FOR JUPITER

Jupiter is the planet of abundance, generosity or over-generosity so that he also rules obesity; great respect for formality, protection when in an angular house, and the bestowal of honors when well aspected to the ruler of the Ascendant. He rules philosophy and all forms of higher wisdom including religion, & also philanthropy. As a rule, he represents wealth.

1. Jupiter in any house increases the number there of whatever that house represents. In the marriage-7th, several marriages; in the mother-10th or in the father-4th, a step-parent or foster parent. In the 11th, many friends; in the 3rd, many blood-relatives and neighbors; in the 5th, many children, and so on.

2. Jupiter in the 10th gives the native great luck in achieving his chosen career, conferring honor and respect. It is the end-of-the-matter-4th for marriage and promises comparative wealth thereby & inheritance or settlement when the marriage ends, usually at the death of the partner rather than by divorce.

If the 3rd House contains a malefic or is ruled by one that is afflicted, denoting the violent death of a relative, Jupiter in the 10th (which is the 8th for that relative) may confer death-honors or medals on that relative - and which may pass to the native.

3. Jupiter is the Greater Benefic and never as bad when afflicted as the other planets can be. He may withhold a portion when retrograde, but not all; and even in adversity he gives hope while there is life.

4. Jupiter in or ruling the 4th gives a large home

and a large family, a generous father and many gifts
from him, unless badly afflicted. It is generally a
religious family or a member is affiliated with some
religious organization. The native has many changes
of address and will not continue at his birthplace.

5.   Jupiter in an angular house (or ruling one) denotes the wearing of a uniform at some time of life.

6.   Jupiter in the 6th House gives digestive upset,
good servants but wasteful, animal pets expensive to
maintain and indulgent habits difficult to overcome.

7.   Jupiter in the 2d, 8th, 9th or 10th, or in Taurus or Sagittarius shows ownership of insurance pol-
icies and also of diplomas or certificates of merit.

8.   Jupiter in or ruling the 9th House or any angle
promises long journeys or voyages not necessarily at
the native's own expense.   Friends are easily made.

9.   Following the so-called #14 Theory, which shows
the effect of a planet in other houses, subtract the
number of the house Jupiter is in from 14 which will
give the number of another house where his influence
will be markedly felt. When in the 1st or 7th House
at birth the same effect continues throughout life –
because subtracting these from 14 returns to the 1st
or 7th House.   Jupiter in the 5th-of-children gives
the probability of many grandchildren because 5 from
14 gives the 9th House (grandchildren) where Jupiter
would thus register.   Why does Jupiter in the ill-
ness-6th make the native think it is all up for him?

10. Jupiter in aspect with other planets brings out
the best the others have to offer. He protects the
chart that is under bad affliction if he is conjunct
or in good aspect to the Ascendant or its ruler.

                    * * * * *

MY NOTEBOOK FOR VENUS

Venus is the natural ruler of the 2nd House which has to do with precedent, custom and tradition, thus it rules heredity: what you bring into life with you and find easiest to express: in other words, talents and innate abilities. She is also natural ruler of the 7th House which has to do with co-operation, cohesion, harmony and peace. Also, she is exalted in the 12th House of enforced submission, obedience and self-abnegation & indulgent pity for human frailty. All of these attributes, including the talents, will be expressed in life through the Sign & House she is in at birth to the extent that she is well aspected.

1. If Venus is not afflicted by the conjunction or bad aspect to Saturn, she is not limited in expressing & enjoying her talents as she wishes. Otherwise she must express her submissive side & accept limitation, renouncing something of the house she is in & still counting her blessings which she does readily.

2. Where you have this "lesser benefic" you will be desirous of co-operating, being obedient to what may be required for the well-being of the people of that house. Venus agrees quickly and is the great reconciler, bringing peace to that department, healing or mending breaches, unobtrusively sharing what she has to give, and always improving the conditions there.

3. Venus rules all kinds of trimmings: lace, braid, ribbons, and especially fringe. Thus, she not only grants the good of the house she is in but also what may be called "fringe benefits" or an added benefit.

4. Because Venus rules ornaments, she is considered "an ornament to society" in that part of the circle.

5. Since she rules the affectional nature Venus reveals that your greatest fondness for people, places and interests lies in the house she is in. You will be happier there and affectionately inclined, & that is where you will find appreciation in return, since Venus seeks to balance the scales justly and evenly.

6. Whether your role in life is public or private, your main audience is in the house your Venus is in.

7. Venus loves that which is genuine and high-grade so that in any house she prefers that which is best. This is particularly evident in cadent houses, where her choice of reading-matter appeals to her "purity" preference - as art, poetry, the drama and religion.

8. Venus-of-rhythm in strong aspect with Saturn-of-timing is conscious of precision to the point of obsession.   Weak aspects merely appreciate precision.

9. Where Venus is by house, there you find a woman who means much to you. She is either a person ruled by that house itself, or one ruled by the house that follows, therefore playing a behind-the-scenes role.

10. Venus and the Moon in good aspect indicate love of home, of the mother and of the country.   The bad aspects shorten the mother's life or affect the home life unfavorably, so far as happiness is concerned.

11. Venus, Mercury and the Sun are never far apart, so that they may be parallel, conjunct, semisextile, semisquare or in mutual reception only, giving more-or-less happiness or peace of mind, love of the arts and at least some education in life.   Births around midday are more fortunate because these three are in elevation in the chart: love, gain and education are sure to be attained, and the health is usually good.

12. Venus conjunct Uranus means love at first sight
and hasty marriage, then separation or divorce. The
square and opposition give trouble with the opposite
sex; the quincunx breaks engagements. Trines, sextiles & parallels grant perfect love & understanding.

13. Venus and Saturn in any aspect will stabilize &
cool the affectional nature towards sentiment rather
than sentimentality, and marriage is entered into in
a level-headed way, sensibly appraising the other's
qualifications. Oppositions signify a leash-hold in
marriage; also the death of loved ones and restraint
of opportunity according to the house Saturn is in -
and usually accounts for being rejected by a parent.

14. Any aspect between Venus and Neptune idealizes
love; and if in angular houses, puts the beloved one
on a pedestal, to be looked-up-to and adored. There
is sheer luck in life -- financial if also in aspect
to gainful-Jupiter or windfall-Uranus or golden-Sun.
The conjunction or any bad aspect brings clandestine
attractions if in cadent houses, & notably the 12th,
especially in horary charts, signifying association.

15. In a horary chart, Venus in the 12th House discloses a sweetheart behind the scenes. If she rules
the 1st or 7th and is in opposition to the ruler of
the 7th or 1st or Saturn it denotes unrequited love.

16. Venus conjunct or well aspected to Mars softens
his brusqueness in return for his enthusiasm. Badly
aspected, an iron hand shows through a velvet glove.

17. Venus is most important in comparing the charts
of two people entering into any association but particularly marriage. The good or bad nature of her
aspect to the other person's planets as given above,
tells what good to expect & what pitfalls to avoid.

★ ★ ★ ★ ★

MY NOTEBOOK FOR NEPTUNE

Neptune is the shadow planet, elusive & delusive, throwing a veil over what is real so that it appears to be more attractive and desirable, more ideal, and mysterious in some way, being as untrue as the alias or assumed identity this planet also rules. Having a falsehood capability, Neptune rules misinformation & subversion, defrauding schemes that collapse, fogs & films, fading away & disappearance. Because it is possessed of great beauty & naive appeal, Neptune is considered by many to be the higher octave of Venus.

1.   Where Neptune is by house, there will you be in danger of being defrauded by persons of that house & at such time that Neptune is transited by progressed or current malefics. Being slow-moving, these bring an extended period of such danger.   Non-malefics do not cause trouble: rather, they denote lucky periods and if both a malefic and a non-malefic are together there, the difficulties will not be so bad (or there will be some form of compensation for the trouble).

2.   The part of the body ruled by the Sign Neptune is in is subject to weakening by a collection of pus or by virus infection, by drugs or alcohol, by fumes and gas, and by congenital weakness or deformity if Neptune is badly afflicted in the 1st or 4th House.

3.   Neptune in an angular house is romantic & some-times attracted to marriage before the wedding, or a mistake in that document comes to light later.   The marriage ends in divorce or the partner's death, and an unusual situation develops in the interim.   There is detachment from relatives, changes of address and possibility of a voyage, sometimes a freak accident.

4.   Neptune in a succeedent house gives danger of a
financial loss through fraud, speculation, unfortunate trust in the partner or spouse, dependence on an
unfavorable Will or false friends; and by robberies.
Denial of children or disappointment in them because
of their actions; miscarriage or abortion probable,
since this is the planet of assassination & suicide.
Alienation from friends or they are seen but seldom.
Unconsciousness at death, which is calm & peaceful.

5.   Neptune in a cadent house gives strange illness
hard to diagnose, addiction to medicines, poisoning,
hospitalization or imprisonment; voyages, elopement,
defrauding of insurance, or through false relatives.
Through accident or age impairment or weakness, this
is the planet of substitute members such as dentures
and glass eyes, wigs, replacement limbs, & so forth.

6.   Anyone born with Neptune conjunct the Sun, Moon
or Mercury must have sound advice from others before
committing himself to an important decision, lest he
make a serious mistake. This is the planet that can
easily-and-often lead the person regrettably astray.

7.   Neptune is the planet of psychic awareness & of
extra-sensory perception. When well aspected in the
1st House or in any aspect except the conjunction to
the Sun, Moon, Mercury, Saturn, Uranus or Jupiter, a
certain recognition of what is "behind the veil" may
be inborn in the native. Such awareness can operate
as continuous clairvoyance or natural trance states,
or when Neptune is illuminated by a progression or a
lunation, or while he himself is changing direction.

8.   In the different Signs, Neptune's effects are a
great deal the same as when in the houses such Signs
rule in the natural wheel.   Cardinal Signs are read
like angular houses, Fixed like succeedent, & so on.

☆ ☆ ☆ ☆ ☆

A CHART FOR THE PARALLEL POINTS

11:38:00 p.m. EST Jan. 19, 1902 74-W 41-N

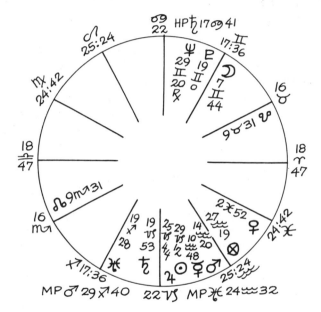

Below medium height, plump, pretty; brown curling hair, brown eyes. Prefers business life to domestic and is secretary to an important personage, carrying most of the family's expenses (after marriage also). Usually robust health but has had several operations relatively major in character. Owns some property.

MY NOTEBOOK FOR URANUS

Uranus is the unpredictable planet which brings things to pass unexpectedly and suddenly, and always with some extraordinary departure from the norm. He stops matters in their tracks, so to say, re-routing them or detouring them contrary to an original plan. His house position shows an unstable foundation that disrupts conditions there where something or someone is not to be depended on to assist or act normally.

ANGULAR: an erratic person dominates the life and there is alienation from the family so that the person withdraws into himself or takes French leave (by running away from home, eloping, etc.). The address undergoes frequent changes, real estate is not often held for life, domestic affairs and routine are frequently disrupted, the employment is unsteady, and a parent was previously divorced. The native himself is somewhat of a genius & different from his family.

SUCCEEDENT: there are unexpected ups and downs in the circumstances; financial affairs are uncertain & possessions are misplaced, lost or stolen. There is loss by speculation, gambling, joint ownerships, and by legacies or settlements denied. Friends are not there when needed; memberships, plans, and hopes and wishes go awry; interest in children, creative work, lovers and research may quickly waver or disappoint.

CADENT: the education lacks continuity, religious beliefs cause estrangement, needed help is generally slow in coming, there are enmities & financial losses through friends, strangers, relatives, inferiors, & tenants. Work is done by fits & starts and under irregular inspiration, and the nervous system gives trouble; there are strange and spasmodic allergies.

Uranus' Parallel POINTS should be noted (they are his distance from his nearest angles taken across to the other side).   In the woman's chart on page 46, Uranus is between the 1st & 4th, his nearest angles, giving his Meridian & Horizontal Parallel Points as:

	S	dg mn		S	dg mn
The I.C.	9	22:00	Uranus	8	19:28
- Uranus	8	19:28	- Ascend	6	18:47
DISTANCE	1	02:32	DISTANCE	2	00:41
Plus I.C.	9	22:00	From Asc	6	18:47
MP Aquar.	(10)	24:32	HP Leo	(4)	18:06

Enter the points outside the wheel as shown here. Any planet coming to the conjunction or opposition of his Meridian or Horizontal Parallel Point forms a parallel to Uranus himself. Since he is a slow-moving planet not registering appreciably by Secondary progression, use the Solar Arc 0:59 per year to progress him (also his Meridian and Horizontal Parallel Points) either directly or conversely, to aspects in the chart.   The number of degrees required to do it discloses the person's age at the time of the event.

In addition, the so-called #14 Theory is valuable in affording further clues to his influence in other houses.   For this, the number of the house he is in is deducted from 14, the remainder being the number of the house which reacts to his influence, and this procedure is also applied to his MP and HP Points. Being Uranus, his influence is generally disruptive.

In this chart Uranus himself in the 3rd reacts in the 11th (14 - 3 = 11), which is the death-8th after the family-4th.   His MP 24 Aquarius in the 4th will be felt in the employment-10th, and his HP 18 Leo in the 10th will react in the domestic-4th.   We expect the unexpected in these departments therefore and we

forecast the year by noting the degrees required for
progressed aspects to culminate. Planets in angular
houses register very strongly in events in the life.

We note that Uranus' MP 24 Aquarius occurs in the
father-4th and Mars there will conjunct it in 10 degrees (10 years) endangering the father's life since
these are both malefics.   He died suddenly (Uranus'
effect in the family-death-11th) in April, 1912, her
age 10 years 3 months converting to Solar Arc 10:06,
which moved Mars to 24:26 Aquarius, conjunct the MP
of Uranus. By this same arc, the Sun ruler 11th in
9 Aquarius squared the nodes, denoting a fatality in
the family because he was in the 4th.   Uranus moved
to 29 Sagittarius conjunct Mars' MP and setting off
its opposition to Neptune so that he died in a coma.

When a child was no longer expected because of an
illness usually precluding pregnancy, the unexpected
happened and on May 3, 1927 her child was born. The
arc for the woman's age was 24:55 which brought the
Sun to 24:07 Aquarius conjunct the Meridian Parallel
of Uranus who rules her 5th-of-children.   The Moon
moved to 2 Cancer, trine Venus in the children-5th.

The astrologer first examined the chart in 1941 &
warned the woman that during 1942 Uranus would conjunct the Sun and cause the loss of an important man
in the family (1942 measuring to age 40, or distance
in degrees between Uranus and the Sun in the family-
4th, a masculine significator of importance). Since
she was married, the Sun represented the husband and
thus widowhood would have to be proved in the chart.

For widowhood, note Venus-ruler-Ascendant in the
widow Sign Pisces & semisquare the marriage-7th cusp
whose ruler Mars is exactly sesquare Neptune, planet
of widows; and the south node in the 7th square Mer-

cury, ruler of the 12th, the house of widowhood.   On
Oct. 4, 1942 her husband died very unexpectedly of a
heart attack without any previous indication of such
disease, even to his doctor who had examined him for
a digestive upset only a month before. Yet the decanate on the husband-7th in the Leo-HEART-area shows
a heart condition, chronic by square to Saturn.   The
arc 40:07 which brought Uranus conjunct the Sun also
brought the Moon who rules her end-of-marriage-10th
to 17:51 Cancer conjunct the HP of Saturn and square
the 7th cusp.   The Sun in 9 Pisces again signified a
fatality by being in the same degree as the nodes.

Sometimes the degrees in the chart correspond to
the person's age at important events. Here, we note
Mercury 10 degrees, and the death of her father when
she was ten. Her marriage lasted from Aug. 10, 1924
to Oct. 4, 1942: 18 years, and 18 degrees on the 7th
cusp. She was age 22 at marriage, the degree on the
domesticity-4th, & age 25 at the birth of the child,
the degree on the children-5th cusp.   For an event
past the 30 degrees allotted to the Signs, we simply
multiply the planetary degrees.   Thus, at widowhood
the arc 40 was four times the degree of Mercury, who
rules the widowhood-12th House, and twenty times the
degree of Venus her ruler in Pisces, Sign of widows.

In the summer of 1948, age 46, arc 45:20, Venus-
ruler-Ascendant moved to 18:12 Aries to conjunct the
marriage-7th cusp and she became engaged.   The 9th
House rules second marriages but the widowhood planet Neptune is there, & Mars-ruler-7th progressed to
29:40 Pisces, the widow Sign, & squared that Neptune
while Venus squared Saturn's HP 17:41 Cancer there &
her fiancé suddenly dropped dead of a heart attack
that summer, making her a widow before she could become a wife again. Neptune himself in 14:40 Leo had
moved to the opposition of Mars-ruler-marriage-7th.

* * * * *

THE NODAL POINTS OF THE PLANETS

Most students of astrology use the Moon's nodes in
natal charts but pay little or no attention to those
of the eight planets, yet these are also of value by
conferring something of their own nature on the person whose planets they conjoin, thus explaining some
of his special leanings to that extent. A planet on
one of these nodes at birth has that nodal vibration
inborn and lasting throughout life, but a progressed
planet there has the vibration only as long as it is
within 1 degree before and 1 degree after that node.

Each planet moves in a circular path or orbit, and
revolves around the Sun in such a way that its orbit
intersects his at two opposite points in the zodiac.
The point in north celestial latitude is called its
North Node: its opposite is the South Node; they are
marked according to the Sign and degree they occupy.
The North Node is Jupiterian in effect, giving more;
the South Node is Saturnian, giving less. The Sun's
path cannot cross itself, thus the Sun has no nodes.

The nodal points of the planets move not more than
a degree and a half in a hundred years. Their North
Nodes in 1960 were approximately:

Mercury -	18 Taurus	Jupiter -	10 Cancer
Mars ----	19 Taurus	Pluto ---	20 Cancer
Uranus --	13 Gemini	Saturn --	23 Cancer
Venus ---	16 Gemini	Neptune -	11 L e o

Venus' nodes are harmonizing, giving easy acquies-
cence by the native in handling the planet's affairs
and making him indulgent, obedient, easily persuaded
toward peaceful solutions & having a romantic urge.

THE DUKE OF WINDSOR

10:00:00 p.m. June 23, 1894, London, England

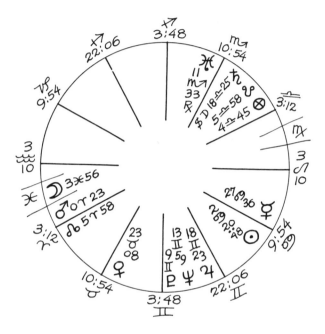

    The natal chart for the Duke of Windsor, romantic in his capacity to give up the throne of England for "the woman I love" has the node of his own ruler Uranus conjunct the idealizing, self-abnegating planet Neptune, signifying an overwhelming devotion. They married on June 3, 1937 with transiting Sun ruler of this marriage-7th conjunct both the Uranian node and Neptune co-ruler of the intercepted Sign in the 1st.

THE DUCHESS OF WINDSOR

5:23:19 a.m. LMT June 19, 1896 - 39N16 76W41

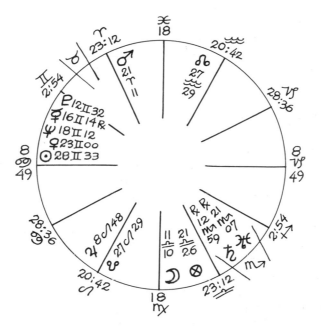

    The Venusian node 16 Gemini conjunct Mercury here
gives charm of voice and a mind attuned to beauty in
any form.   The Duchess would make an interior decor-
ator of distinction if she chose, since these are in
close conjunction to Neptune, higher octave of Venus
(artistry, especially interior decoration) and ruler
of the career-10th here; and Mercury is the ruler of
cleverness and interpretation, however expressed.

Saturn's nodes are diplomatic, tactful, practical
and conscientious, dispensing with non-essentials, &
never letting go of what he thinks has value. He is
said to practise what Jupiter preaches - Jupiter who
recommends foresight, then gives his valuables away.

The Duke's reputation for diplomacy in speech
is well-founded with Saturn's tactful node exactly sextile Venus from Mercury's vicinity: &
Saturn in the 8th dispenses with his "natural"
legacy by giving up his non-essential right to
the throne & so relinquishing its perquisites,
rather than relinquish the more-valuable love.

Jupiter's node broadens the scope and pushes into
the future. The native observes the formalities and
preaches the highest ethics in handling the planet's
affairs and has a degree of protection in adversity.

Jupiter's node on the Duke's 6th cusp broadens
the sphere of service he gives & receives. At
age 7 his progressed Sun reached this cusp at
the accession to the throne of his grandfather
Edward VII, under whose name he himself was to
accede to the throne as Edward VIII, thus continuing his service as David, Prince of Wales,
until a family death made him King. His ruler
Saturn in the 8th gives position through death
of another, and exactly trine Jupiter ruler of
his career-10th broadened the scope so that a
greater title was included. At the same time,
his progressed Sun selected his future "queen"
by exactly conjuncting the Duchess' Ascendant.

The Uranian node aids in finding the best way out
of a dilemma or the answer to a problem even when it
means disruption of existing conditions and severing
of bonds: it is politically-minded and interested in

memberships and other adoptive affiliations. Such a
planet's affairs are expressed in ways that are new,
different, universal in application, and with humane
intent, & there is always a departure from the norm.

GEORGE VI, KING OF ENGLAND

1:20:06 a.m. June 3, 1865, London, England

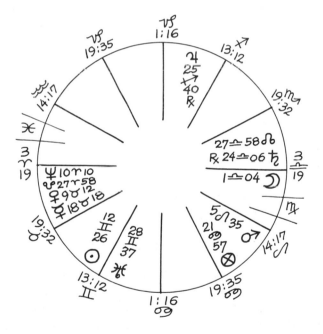

The King's chart shows the Uranian node conjunct
the Sun. By royal decree in 1917 he changed the name

of the Royal House from Saxe-Coburg (of Germany) to
Windsor. This was a disorganizing, political & far-
sighted move of universal interest because he thereby freed his family from their large group of German
affiliations by taking the best way out of a dilemma
involving an inimical nation during World War times.

Uranus himself permits the right answer to any
problem connected with the 3rd House simply by
being there (brethren, decisions, etc.) and he
married Mary, fiancée of his brother Clarence
who died during their engagement.   This was a
wise answer, making for a very happy marriage.

The Neptunian nodes have an extraordinary, sheer-
luck, beyond-the-law vibration flouting conventional
methods of dealing with the planet they conjoin; and
there is the possibility of extra-sensory perception
with flashes of insight or hunches that turn out to
be correct, successful, but abnormal or destructive.

In the Duchess' chart, the Neptunian node conjunct Jupiter in Leo, ruler of her career-10th
and in her possession-2nd, meant extraordinary
sheer luck in bringing exalted position, title
& magnificent possessions, together with great
wealth. With Jupiter square Saturn, ruler 8th
in the 5th-of-children, however, the abnormal,
abortive vibration would deny motherhood - and
this was true and confirmed by Venus-ruler-5th
conjunct Neptune & exactly semisquare Jupiter.
At their marriage, the Duke's Sun had left his
5th-of-children and was conjunct the Neptunian
node 11 Leo square his natal Uranus, which was
an ominous denial of children from that union.

With Mercury's nodes, the native handles the matters of the planet with speed and dexterity, clever-

ness or shrewdness, usually involving a document and often acting as go-between, agent or representative.

The King had Mercury's node on Mercury himself in the 1st House, giving MASTERLY ability when acting for others in a personal way, as he did in marrying his brother's fiancée, in changing the family name and in sponsoring the Daylight Saving Bill (documentary) which he did in 1916 during his reign, all "go-between" activities.

With Mars' nodes, the native exhibits technical & mechanical aptitude, enterprise, dynamic push, & enthusiasm in engineering the planet's affairs - often with daring or recklessness but always courageously.

The King's Mercury on Mars' North Node denotes a quick temper and the capacity to express it. The Duchess has Uranus conjunct the South Node of Mars in the 5th of anything that is speculative in the way it will turn out (children or love-affairs, gambling, etc.) and she was very "courageous" in daring to take chances here.

Pluto's nodes bring a personal waywardness in expressing or developing the planet's interests from a seemingly-unrelated beginning to a position that may set it apart, without the usual connected procedure: much as a melody is taken from its original source & put to unrelated use such as the Salvation Army hymn "Onward, Christian Soldiers" which had its source in a Gilbert & Sullivan operetta, sans religious basis.

The King's Fortuna in the children-5th is conjunct Pluto's node, setting his children apart & isolating them in some way; as when his son, the Duke, and his daughter Princess Mary, married commoners, a form of royal waywardness.

✹ ✹ ✹ ✹ ✹

Aspect	Distance	Orb
conjunction	00 together ..	8
semisextile	30 dg apart ..	2
SEMIQUINTILE ...	36 " ..	1
SEMISQUARE	45 " ..	4
sextile	60 " ..	8
QUINTILE	72 " ..	2
square	90 " ..	8
TRECILE	108 " ..	2
trine	120 " ..	8
SESQUARE	135 " ..	4
BIQUINTILE	144 " ..	2
QUINCUNX	150 " ..	2
opposition	180 " ..	8
PARALLEL	same declin. ..	1

For the Parallel, both planets may
be in North Declination or both in
South Declination, operating like a
conjunction in cooperative effect.
One North and the other South has a
threat of separation in the future.

Other Relationships

MUTUAL RECEPTION (each planet in the other's
natural Sign). No orb of aspect is required
in this relationship but we use the relation
by Signs and note whether they are in opposition, trine, square, sextile, and so forth.

MUTUAL APPLICATION to the aspect: one moving
forward and the other retrograding to their
aspect. A great orb is allowed because they
are working together to reduce the distance.

HOW DO YOU LIKE BEING AN EARTHLING?

At the time of your birth the Sun was in a certain
Sign while the Earth itself was in the opposite Sign
so that you are a spiritual entity born into a physical environment that is closer than close, like the
body you inhabit.   This closeness is not because of
the Earth but because of conditions on its surface
which form what we call the World.   It is important
that we recognize this differentiation between the
globe on which we live & the conditions under which
we operate.   Though the Earth endure forever, the
World will not only come to an end but does so every
time an empire falls or the stock market crashes or,
to bring it nearer home, any drastic development in
our personal life makes us start a new chapter following a loss: our little world comes to an end, and
new conditions arise for us to live through.   The
Earth's symbol ⊕ is her circle enclosing her meridian and horizon -- differing from Fortuna's symbol ⊗
whose cross marks the financial (succeedent) houses.

You are to find equilibrium as an Earthling, and
particularly as regards the worldly requirements you
face, which are based on the conditions into which
you are born. You have to get along with others and
adapt yourself to situations, face reality, and complete your mission on Earth with credit to yourself,
according to the handicap that you may expect to be
born under - human imperfection. This you do to the
extent that the planetary rulers of your Sun Sign &
the opposite Earth Sign are in aspect, to indicate
interaction between you and surrounding conditions.

We must always take into account the extra aspects
available, shown in capital letters on the opposite
page, revealing a usually-unrecognized relationship.

For the aspects having an 8-degree orb the Sun and
Moon are allowed an orb of 10 degrees.   These are
never retrograde - in reality, neither are the other
bodies, which only seem to be going backward because
of the Earth's changing speed of motion in her orbit
and the slower speed of the planet in its own orbit.
However, since it is the Earth that is primarily the
instigator, and your physical body is "of the earth,
earthy" it follows that there will be a physical sig-
nificance to anything of an indirect nature in your
chart.   Direct planets show RESPONSE to conditions:
retrograde planets show REACTION which, being indirect, operates mainly on the inner plane but is still
engendered by environmental causes if the planet has
rulership of the Earth Sign opposite your Sun Sign.

Chart for Benito Mussolini

1:37:48 pm LMT July 29, 1883 - Dovia, Italy, 12E 44N

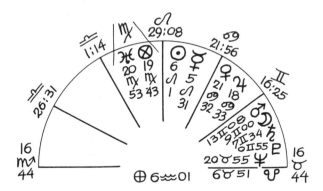

Here, the Earth in Aquarius has two rulers, denoting two kinds of environmental conditions which will
be met as part of his mission on Earth because they
are both aspected by the Sun, ruling his birth Sign.

His ruler Sun sextile Saturn is very good to raise
him to greatness in the world since the Sun is ruler
of the Midheaven, his career and high position. The
Earth at his birth therefore provided worldly conditions to his advantage, admirable or not. To confirm this we find Saturn's dispositor Mercury in Leo
the kingly Sign, so that he bore the title of Duce.

The Sun semisquare to Uranus is very bad, however,
casting him down from the highest house to the worst
ignominy possible - that of being murdered (Mars and
Uranus square) and his naked corpse hung upside down
in public for the rabble to jeer at and spit on.

For confirmation of this, the Sun is quintile his
own Solstice Point 24 Taurus, which is not only ill-
starred by being exactly conjunct Caput Algol, which
is considered to be the most evil fixed star of all,
but is also exactly conjunct the Part of Death (the
Ascendant plus the 8th cusp and then minus the Moon)
signifying a violent death. Scorpio rising is often
indicative of embarrassment through being seen nude.

Aries people always have help from others because
at their birth the Earth is in the most co-operative
Sign of all, Libra, showing benefic world conditions
facing them because the ruler is Venus.   The better
she appears in the chart, the better the conditions.
People born in the last decanate of Leo are similar-
ly blessed because they face the Libra decanate of
Aquarius. Those born in the middle decanate of Sagittarius face the Libra decanate of Gemini, thereby
receiving aid in life. The ratio rises or falls according to aspects, but life is always made easier
than otherwise for these natives, and any misfortune
will be counterbalanced by some compensation - which
was not the case with Mussolini: for one thing, his
Leo Sun did not face the Libra decanate of Aquarius.

Planets retrograde at your birth show that you use
their power INDIRECTLY, and if the ruler of your Sun
Sign or Earth Sign is retrograde in your chart, then
you are inclined toward indirection too, in handling
world conditions, either because you want to or have
to.   If well-placed by Sign, or in mutual reception
(which gives "exchange" status) you use diplomacy in
settling affairs with others to mutual satisfaction.

In passing, retrograde planets reveal something of
the house they are in that you keep to yourself - or
will not discuss & are reluctant to accept or admit,
and if they are malefics it is serious.   They often
represent a person of that house rejected, sent away
or turned out of doors, disinherited, or put out of
your circle: you, yourself, may be rejected by him.

Having no planets retrograde at birth, Mussolini could take advantage of the opportunities
the world promised him by the Sun ruler of his
career-10th sextile Saturn ruler of the Earth,
and he would do so arrogantly because of being
"born to the purple" with the Sun in the regal
Sign Leo.   Success would come all the easier.

If a natal planet goes retrograde after birth however, it marks a somewhat similar effect in the life
until it goes direct - which it may not do within a
reasonable number of days after birth corresponding
altogether to age 100, if we are optimists.   If it
happens to rule the Earth Sign there will be a withholding of worldly benefits for the duration; otherwise the effect continues for life in a lesser sense
than if natally retrograde.   If it backs into a better Sign it may prove more beneficial in some way. A
malefic turning retrograde by progression times the
passing away of someone important to you: if it is a
benefic, something inanimate passes out of your hold

or keeping, such as a possession or favored position
and so forth. A planet turning in either direction
signals a change from the previous condition in that
house. In the 6th or 12th House, those going direct
take a turn for the better in sickness or misfortune
but those going retrograde take a turn for the worse
or repeat some undesirable symptom or trouble. In a
Fixed Sign, the condition becomes established and if
it rules the Earth Sign it affects worldly standing.

Mussolini's Saturn went retrograde in 1939 accounting for his change in prestige from 1938,
the year of his conquest in Africa, and public
opinion now went against him. As Mercury went
retrograde in 1941 his kingly position took a
turn for the worse, which led to his enforced
resignation in 1943 when Mercury reached Libra
21:32R and completed the square to Venus ruler
of his contacts-7th & semisquare natal Saturn.

Transiting planets are those in the current ephemeris: they come from outside your natal chart, thus
outsiders come into your circle with their personal
affairs, in more or less temporary association with
you as they reach your natal or progressed planets.
Also, if a transit turns either retrograde or direct
conjunct itself in your natal chart it is identified
with your life at the time according to whatever the
planet represents (Mercury, communication in all its
forms: Mars, enterprise: Venus, social advancement &
reconciliations, and so on). If turning direct, it
is your signal to go ahead but if turning retrograde
you are cautioned to proceed warily: worldly affairs
will not go well, especially if it is the Earth Sign
ruler that is being transited in your natal chart.

In Mussolini's chart, transiting Venus who was
direct at birth turned retrograde August 1943,

conjunct natal Uranus in the 10th House.   In
the following month transiting Uranus turned
retrograde conjunct natal Saturn.   In December
transiting Jupiter turned retrograde conjunct
the Midheaven.   Thus, his 10th cusp and 10th-
house planet and the rulers of his Earth Sign
were all involved in misfortune because of the
retrograde transit of natally-direct planets.
As an earthling, the world turned against him
because he did not proceed warily, being arro-
gant, and his affairs went wrong: and this co-
incided with his enforced resignation in 1943.

In day-to-day use of this work it is therefore the
part of wisdom to keep an eye on the ruler of your
Earth Sign, marking any transit that is to change in
direction there, and especially if retrograding.   At
such times use more discretion than usual in affairs
in general, since they are bound to undergo a change
accordingly, that you are thus warned of in advance.

If your Earth Sign ruler was not strong enough at
birth to provide worldly advantages beyond the ordinary, do not tempt Providence by flying too high and
falling too low in the world: be happy with what you
can reach safely - and in that way you may find that
being an Earthling is infinitely more to your liking
because it carries more security.   You can always
rise in YOUR world without having to be a Mussolini.

* * * * *

Venus, Uranus & Saturn in the 7th House

I met her but a short time since,
    Yet knew at once that I
Would hold her ever in my heart,
    And love her 'til I die.

* * * * *

THE SHAPE YOU ARE IN

If you could take off your skin and sit around in your bones, the pattern of your life's framing would show up at once, with Saturn the most evident of all your planets because he rules the skeletal framework and, by extension, your basic pattern in all things. To recognize your inherent pattern or the shape your life is framed in you must look to your natal Saturn therefore, noting which ANGULAR house he is already in or first enters by transit as he goes through the Signs either direct or retrograde, after your birth.

When actually achieved and thus in your 1st, 4th, 7th or 10th House - the ones that give shape to your wheel of life - then the pattern is considered to be shaped by the nature of that house and he throws two squares and an opposition to the remaining three, to modify your pattern accordingly. The angle he is in has the effect of a conjunction and makes matters of that house basic in your fundamental urges. The two houses that are square show where obstacles lie, and where too-zealous efforts to establish a pattern may react in loss, undue expense or much disappointment. The angle in opposition shows the non-cooperation or separative influence to be faced in maintaining your pattern. An opposition however is like a full Moon: you are fully aware of the conditions you face & can see clearly, since you have a light in the darkness.

When we deal with an empty house we read it as an outside or world condition into which we are born on the planet Earth. Planets in houses, however, bring those affairs down to earth so to speak where Saturn must wrestle with them by mundane HOUSE conjunction, square or opposition in developing the basic pattern even though they are as yet in aspect only by house.

It is essential that you accept your pattern with understanding if you are to develop its best points. If Saturn is well placed by Sign (Capricorn, Aquarius, Libra, or any Earth or Air Sign, or is in mutual reception with another planet (each in the Sign that the other rules) which gives him status as though in his own Sign of dignity, then instead of reacting to the exigencies of bad mundane aspects he responds by handling them with diplomacy, tact & patient waiting so that the pattern eventually emerges as it should. This type of Saturn is the good and kind Teacher who knows what the native requires to improve his field.

If your natal Saturn is weakly placed by being in his detriment in Cancer or his fall in Aries and not in mutual reception, then difficulties arise in life to delay or deny the best opportunities at the right time to develop your pattern. You are forced to bow the head and bend the knee in dealing with the planets in square or opposition, recognizing Saturn as a Taskmaster, because you react instead of responding. The moment you stop wrestling with him and learn his lesson you learn the way to achieve your pattern and you are a nobler person than otherwise, because your character reflects the grace of humility rather than resignation, and the power of adjustment to reality.

When the natal Saturn is in a Sign to which he is unrelated in any way, good or bad, he is peregrine - that is, aimless: wandering, off the beam or without purpose in life - and needs squares to galvanize him into action towards establishing a pattern. He will of course be saved if in mutual reception so that he eventually builds an acceptable pattern thru others. This type of Saturn is the hardest to handle or follow in establishing a pattern because of the lack of a driving force. Success comes from accepting it as a dare, a challenge to fight a lackadaisical absence

of ambition or industry, and your best weapon is the
strongest aspect he makes or receives in your chart.
The strongest is a conjunction or parallel, then the
square, the semisquare and sesquare and opposition -
especially if the Ascendant is included. A sextile
brings him an opportunity but a lackadaisical Saturn
doesn't usually bestir himself to reflect his opportunities in life. Trines make it too easy for peregrine planets to accept something unearned for which
payment must be made later. Trines coming from our
non-peregrine planets show what we earned previously
and now enjoy and express easily as talent & genius.

Saturn rules PLANS because, like a skeleton, they
are architectural & basic in their reason for being.
If it is the 1st House he is in or enters, you make
your plans very early in life knowing from the first
what your pattern is to be and how to mold it; it is
usually a personal endeavor that you try to develop,
and the pattern is in danger of being thwarted somewhat by your mate, an open enemy, the public or public service of some kind that interrupts a personal
plan, due to being opposite the 7th House - and more
surely if there is a planet there to "bring you down
to earth" by its opposition to Saturn-the-practical.

Saturn in or entering the 4th House makes you put
the family first; your pattern takes shape according
to tradition or to noblesse oblige (what is expected
of you). You follow prescribed principles and build
up an estate thereby, usually without parental help,
because in the 4th and opposed by the success-10th.
It is his mundane (house) square to the 1st that may
galvanize you into taking practical action yourself.

In the 7th House Saturn removes you as far as you
can get from the strictly personal; you defer to the
other person dealt with & follow his lead or example

in forming your own pattern & submerge your identity
to great extent: your pattern is largely his and you
therefore merit less credit for what you do and what
you are - which is your own fault because you separate yourself from yourself by being in opposition to
the 1st House, thus operating to your own discredit.

In the 10th, a plan may take longer to formulate,
and may fall by the wayside before your pattern sol-
idifies because Saturn squares the 1st House and can
fall from a great height when highest in the figure.
It will have to do with your career & the reputation
you'build up and also with the stuff that dreams are
made of (because it is the substance-2nd of the 9th-
of-dreams). It may take shape through the influence
of a parent, a superior or dignitary you respect, or
an ecclesiastical or academic figure when Saturn enters from the 9th - or even through the influence of
a stranger or foreigner or in-law, also ruled by the
9th - or because of a friend or club-member, if Saturn retrogrades into the 10th from the 11th. Family
opposition from the 4th may render the pattern somewhat less than completely developed, unless there is
mutual reception to let you circumvent a difficulty.

When Saturn starts from a cadent house (or from a
succeedent through a cadent house to reach an angle)
there is a carry-over of influence accordingly which
shows up sooner or later in the pattern. The cadent
houses have a tendency to infringe on one's freedom,
to hold one back or deny full measure of credit, and
the pattern shows a trait of abnegation or sacrifice
of early opportunity because the person permits himself to be imposed-on unduly. He accepts denial and
assumes another's responsibility or is unfairly pre-
vented from taking advantage of normal opportunities
in life, and his pattern betrays it. Some karma may
be expected to afflict the best pattern-development.

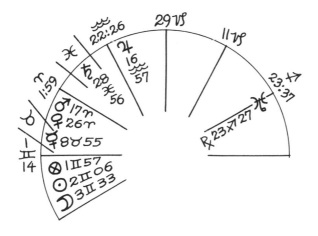

In Queen Victoria's chart shown here, Saturn enters the 1st House angle by transit after birth & thereby sets her pattern early in life: it would be personal in that she would be the main figure, and she would know definitely "from the First" what she was to be, and that she would have to shape her pattern herself as one standing alone. Saturn in the First House is indicative of one to whom sorrow is no stranger.

Born Alexandrina Victoria, she became Victoria I, Queen of Great Britain and Ireland, at age 18. When Saturn entered the 1st in dual-Gemini giving another name, another beginning, another life & another outlook, he also trined the Greater Benefic Jupiter who in the 10th House promised her the greatest position attainable in life - sovereignty. Before that, however, Saturn was forced to go through the jail-12th, and her 18 years were spent in virtual incarceration by her mother, in whose room she always slept and in whose constant presence only was she allowed to converse with anyone: friend, tutor, servant or others.

This seclusion-influence of the 12th House became part and parcel of her character, carrying-over into

her life's pattern so that she went into a voluntary
seclusion of many years, mourning the passing of her
adored husband Albert, the Prince Consort. That her
marriage would prove extremely happy is shown by the
Greater Benefic Jupiter in the 10th House which, being the end-of-the-matter-4th for the marriage-7th,
shows how a marriage will turn out.   Venus, the Sun
or Fortuna in the 10th also bring marital happiness.

Sagittarius, the "foreign" Sign, on the 7th cusp,
is one indication of marriage to one born in another
country, as he was.   His ruler Jupiter is in mutual
reception with the malefic Uranus who is directly on
the cusp of the house of death so that she was fated
to become a widow. She banished Rudyard Kipling for
referring unhappily to her as the Widow of Windsor.

Being a 1st-House pattern, everything would be of
intensely personal importance to her: she would also
register strongly and regally with others around her
and in her world-wide circle, despite the fact that
she was inclined to reticence, was not commanding to
the eye (in fact, was under five feet tall) and may
have discomforted others by her continual grieving.

When Saturn entered her 1st House, in the letter-
writing Sign Gemini, he trined the publishing-planet
Jupiter in her career-10th House, and both of these
became part of the Queen's basic pattern of personal
self-expression.   It is said that she wrote between
500 and 600 bound volumes of long, personal letters.

Her long reign of sixty-four years may be attrib-
uted to the fact that Saturn ruled her 10th-of-rank,
setting the noteworthy pattern when in the 1st House
trine to Jupiter, the great protector, in the 10th.

✵ ✵ ✵ ✵ ✵

WHAT YOU WANT AND WHETHER YOU GET IT

In a natal or horary chart it is always interesting to determine what it is that the person wants, & also whether or not he is going to get it - at least in part if not wholly. WHAT is wanted is denoted by the 11th House of Hopes, Wishes & Circumstances, and WHETHER it is achieved is shown by the planet ruling the Sign on the cusp of the 11th House. Be sure to note the distinction we make here.

An intercepted Sign in the 11th signifies another great desire but of secondary importance and usually held in abeyance because of circumstances over which the person has insufficient control. Sometimes this discloses a future desire still to be formulated.

Fire Signs on the 11th cusp have a basic desire for spiritual things: whatever touches the heart and soul and is creative. Earth Signs want the practical and material, safeguarding type of thing that can be developed into a future security: they want roots in solid ground and something they can hold on to. Air Signs want whatever is intellectual and scientific - the impersonal interests that can logically be given to people in general, because Air Signs are diffuse, having only a light hold on what they want when they get it, especially in matters intellectual, desiring to spread their knowledge: they are teachers. Water Signs want to satisfy their extra-sensory perception through deep understanding of the mystical: whatever appeals to the imagination, feelings and emotions as in things taken on faith: the idealistic, dramatic & poetic or musical, gratifying their hunger for something unworldly, usually withheld and withdrawn from humans, and that can be enjoyed without company. An intercepted Sign adds its element-characteristics.

The Sign on the 11th cusp & any intercepted there
may be ruled by one or more planets. We look to the
house or houses in which they are found in the chart
to determine the departments of life where the hopes
and wishes are being sought - and the more houses we
have to deal with, the more diversified the desires.
The thing to notice specifically is the RELATIONSHIP
of such a house to the 11th House itself, since some
will be square, some trine, and so on -- which tells
us whether the ruler of the 11th there will find conditions easy to handle or not, in gaining his hopes.

The 5th OPPOSES the 11th, denoting that your circumstances involve opposition & non-cooperation from
others who hold you back to that extent so that success is difficult or out of your easy reach. An opposition represents anything that is as far from you
at birth as possible, such as marriage for example -
you have to grow up before you can attain it. On the
other hand, an opposition is like a full moon light-
ing whatever is before you: everything is clear, and
you are aware of what you have to face in life. You
always have to break a bond to overcome oppositions,
and your dearest wish often comes true late in life.

The 4th and 6th are QUINCUNX to the 11th: circumstances have to undergo a radical reorganization before you can attain what you want.   The quincunx is
basically the distance from the Ascendant to the 6th
and also from the 8th to the Ascendant: you must use
great discrimination and a process of elimination in
deciding what it is you want most, so that you don't
put out a worthy effort for an unworthy cause (6th):
or someone has to move out of your way (8th) permitting reorganization of circumstances toward success.

The quincunx can force you to pay another's debts
or put out money for his support or bail, and so on.

The 3rd and 7th are TRINE the 11th: circumstances are felicitous and make it easy to get what you want through relatives, partners, children & appreciative strangers, or by removal to another neighborhood, or even to a foreign country because the original meas- urement of the trine falls between the Ascendant and the 5th and 9th Houses.   It is the luckiest aspect, bringing gain with little effort if any on your part as by 9th-House Divine Intervention in your behalf.

The 2nd and 8th SQUARE the 11th putting obstacles in your way due to circumstances that are frequently financial in character.   You either have too little to begin with or spend too much to aid someone else, all of which means you are financially unprepared to further your own desires properly - so that you make up for it by working harder than is normal. Squares make you go to extremes of effort and since they are basically the distance between the Ascendant and the 4th and 10th, your difficulties may be fundamentally due to family restrictions, or parental inability to provide whatever you need, especially in early life.

The 1st and 9th SEXTILE the 11th. Opportunities, like the postman, will always knock twice, affording excellent chances of success through your own effort or that of people you talk to - since the sextile is basically the distance from the Ascendant to the 3rd (speech & circulation of ideas) & also from the 11th itself (whatever is opportune, arriving well-timed).

The 10th and 12th are SEMISEXTILE to the 11th, so that circumstances favor gaining some of your hopes and wishes, although not as many as through the sex- tile, and not as easily. A semisextile is basically the distance between the Ascendant & the 2nd or 12th (what is coming and what has gone - Future and Past) or only half a chance, because of personal mistakes.

The 11th may be said to CONJUNCT itself, and when
the ruler of the 11th is there it means that circumstances are with you: your hopes & wishes are within
easy grasp and life favors you in attaining whatever
you want almost by wishing it to be so. Friends are
there when needed to accede to your wishes. If the
Sun rules the 11th and is in the 11th and there is a
planet in the 2nd in either a natal or horary chart,
note the date when the Sun conjuncts that planet (by
natal progression or horary transit) because that is
when you are to get something you have long desired.

The ruler of the 11th in MUTUAL RECEPTION (two in
each other's natural Sign) has exchange status & may
be read also as though back in its own Sign, keeping
the same degree. This signifies a change in circumstances permitting you to achieve what you desire by
changing places: getting out of that department, and
into the department where the ruler's degree would
put it (which can be the 11th, 10th or 12th House).

If the ruler of the 11th is RETROGRADE it reveals
that you really don't want whatever it is as much as
you think you do - and you may back down and give up
the whole idea - or promising circumstances may fail
to transpire completely by withholding some detail.

If the ruler of the 11th is STATIONARY it denotes
that matters will be at a standstill temporarily (in
later life in a natal chart: at present, in a horary
chart) due to circumstances affecting your hopes and
wishes related to the house the planet is in. Since
it will go either direct or retrograde there will be
a change thereafter; and the good or bad aspect that
the planet makes to the Ascendant or its ruler tells
whether the change will be for the better or worse -
as applied to the native or the querent in a horary.

* * * * *

THE PLANET THAT TOUCHES YOUR LIFE TODAY

One of the fascinating by-lanes in your chart has to do with the planet that represents your age for a given year-between-birthdays, influencing by its own power whatever progressions are in force at the time and whether or not those progressions involve that age-planet itself.   Each planet has its number, as:

```
1 - S u n      4 - Saturn    7 - Mercury
2 - M o o n    5 - M a r s   8 - Uranus
3 - V e n u s  6 - Jupiter   9 - Neptune
```

Your present age plus your next age REDUCED TO A SINGLE DIGIT gives one of these numbers & thus tells you which planet in your chart will register in your experiences during the period between birthdays: for example, your last birthday 21 plus your next 22 add up to 43 which reduces to 7 and points to Mercury in your chart. Now, what happened of importance to you last year? What was your age-period?   Which planet ruled that period - & wasn't its main characteristic quite distinguishable in what happened at that time?

```
1 S u n     0/1  9/10 18/19 27/28, etc.
3 Venus     1/2 10/11 19/20 28/29,
5 Mars      2/3 11/12 20/21 29/30,
7 Mercury   3/4 12/13 21/22 30/31,
9 Neptune   4/5 13/14 22/23 31/32,
2 Moon      5/6 14/15 23/24 32/33,
4 Saturn    6/7 15/16 24/25 33/34,
6 Jupiter   7/8 16/17 25/26 34/35,
8 Uranus    8/9 17/18 26/27 35/36, etc.
```

A man with the natal Moon in the 3rd House (blood relatives) square Neptune (aspect & planet malefic) lost a grandmother at the Moon-period age 5, and his

father at the Moon-period age 41/42 & a half-brother
at the Moon-period age 59/60 - all during major progressions to other points from other planets. The
age-periods ruled by the Moon must always register
thus for him because of her natal square to Neptune.

Planets direct in motion, unafflicted by malefics
or well-aspected by benefics, strong by Sign or else
in mutual reception with another planet (each in the
other's natural Sign, which gives "exchange status"
& allows the native to get out of what he gets into)
are fortified in your favor. You can always rely on
your fortified planets to protect your interests: it
is the badly-afflicted ones that are suspect, & particularly during their special periods, when they do
not need to be included in any aspect at all at the
time of an event - they are simply in a position at
birth to take part in whatever happens under a major
progression elsewhere if they rule that period.   If
it is a fortunate development by progression a well-
fortified period-ruler may augment the good fortune.

On the opposite page we have the badly-afflicted
chart of a brilliant man deserving of a better fate.
We have a double reason for using his chart: besides
noting the rulers of the periods it also gives us an
unusual opportunity to study the effect of the Part
of Peril when on the Ascendant and square a malefic.

Any chart with Capricorn on the 8th cusp has the
Part of Peril (P) exactly conjunct the Ascendant because the rule is: the 1st plus the ruler of the 8th
and then minus Saturn - which adds and subtracts the
same planet and leaves the Ascendant intact for (P).
If not square a malefic, it is minor in its effect.
If afflicted as here but with some saving grace such
as the conjunction to Venus here although semisquare
Jupiter, there is help in adversity & sorely needed.

AN ACCIDENT-PRONE CHART

1:58:00 a.m. LMT Aug. 11, 1908, 90W12 38N38

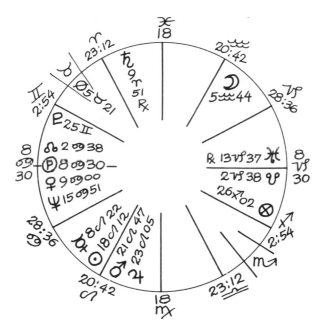

Here, Saturn's square & Uranus' opposition to the Ascendant and (P) operate from angles, meaning major danger in public places and on the street (confirmed by Mars-of-danger in the traffic-3rd semisquare both the Ascendant and (P). Compounding the danger, the Moon his ruler squares Lilith, a sinister influence in the 11th (circumstances out of his control), par-

allels Neptune and opposes Mercury who is in a Fixed
Sign. This affects his mental processes because she
rules the 1st House of the brain and is besieged between major malefics, Uranus and Saturn, who afflict
each other: thus the three mental significators, the
Moon, Mercury and Uranus, are critically afflicted.

Up to age 26 he was possessed of an exceptionally
high IQ, training for the engineering & electronics
fields in which he showed great aptitude. The year
1934 was the culmination of a series of accidents, a
period ruled by Uranus (see Uranus for age 26/27, on
page 75), which stopped him in his tracks so far as
further mental application was concerned, because he
sustained severe head and brain injury at that time.

As in forecasting the future of any chart, we begin with the aspects to culminate earliest & strongest after birth: if they involve the Ascendant, they
involve the native personally & usually physically.
Some astrologers consider this the best way to avoid
forecasting for a future that may never materialize,
but human judgment being not only what it is but
also what it isn't, we should always look for the
saving grace in an afflicted chart, thereby making
fewer mistakes in reading, & specifically as regards
the 8th House, which rules many losses besides the
loss of life: loss of limb by surgery, for instance.

In this regard, all the year-periods whose rulers
are unafflicted in your chart designate the years in
which you are safe to that extent.   Venus & Jupiter
in good aspect to the Ascendant or conjunct the age-
ruler accord saving grace in time of danger.   Venus
on the Ascendant in this chart saves the native from
the worst during periods ruled by Saturn, Uranus and
Neptune who endanger the Ascendant.   A long life is
often signified by the ruler of the 8th retrograde,

saying that Death holds back; by benefics angular or
conjunct the Sun or the Ascendant or its ruler, & by
the North Node on the Ascendant side of the chart.

The first affliction to culminate in this chart
should occur soon after birth, at age 0/1 in the Sun
period, because Saturn immediately squares the First
cusp and the Part of Peril there. The Sun's period
is always afflictive here because he is conjunct and
parallel the malefic Mars, but his conjunction to a
benefic, Jupiter, gives saving grace, resulting in a
knock-down-and-pick-up combination. At age 3 weeks,
a visiting child pulled him off his bed to the floor
and knocked his head badly there, stunning him. In
the head Sign Aries, Saturn denotes falls & injuries
to the head. His mutual square to Venus who is conjunct the comatose planet Neptune accounts for stunning him while saving. By house, the Sun conjunct
the CUSP of the 3rd is always on the BRINK of danger
because Mars is there: on the SIDE of the street and
on the EDGE of anything: at age 3 weeks, the edge of
the bed. Thus (again during the Sun period) in 1917
at age 18/19 he was knocked down by an automobile as
he rode his bicycle on the SIDE of the road, suffering a gashed forehead requiring several stitches. At
that time, the Ascendant was conjunct Neptune, & the
Moon 9 Gemini was conjunct the midpoint between Saturn-of-falls in Aries-the-head & Mercury-of-sewing.

The progressed Moon opposed Mars in a Fire Sign &
semisquared the Ascendant in 1909 at age 1/2 when he
burned both hands horribly on a gas-range. This was
Venus' age-period: conjunct marring-Neptune, he was
saved but disfigured - by fire, due to Mars in Leo.

MARS is not afflicted by malefics, therefore his
periods do not denote years of danger in themselves.
Mars conjunct Jupiter at birth endangers the periods

of Jupiter who is thus conjunct a malefic; while the periods of Mars are protected by his conjunction to a benefic. This also softens the effect of any progressed affliction to Mars - as just noted for 1909.

MERCURY'S only affliction to a malefic is a weak semisquare to Pluto, so his periods would be characterized by only weak participation in any major progression in force at the time and would involve only minor annoyance & discomfort, also minor assistance.

The MOON at birth is not afflicted by malefics so her periods do not denote injurious participation in what takes place under major progressions elsewhere. It is _her_ progressed aspect, especially the conjunction, square or opposition to a malefic that can set off his bad aspects again & again as she goes around the chart, contacting each malefic at least twice.

NEPTUNE is afflicted by square to Saturn & opposition to Uranus. In 1912 he was knocked down and run over by a boy on a bicycle. His whole body was badly bruised, his left eyelid partly torn off, and he was unconscious for hours. The major progression of Sun conjunct Mars in the 3rd was enough to precipitate a dangerous accident in the street, but unlikely to be fatal so close to Jupiter. It was the simultaneous major progression Moon-conjunct-Saturn-square-Uranus and-Neptune that could knock him down and mangle and stun him, this being at age 4 in the Neptune period.

SATURN is afflicted by square to Uranus & Neptune but not until age 33 did a major progression occur in his period so that he could participate. In 1941 progressed Mercury in 9 Libra opposed Saturn, and he suffered gradual deterioration of nerve tissues and loss of hair (ruled by Mercury & Saturn), & was subject to seizures (Saturn square Uranus and Neptune).

JUPITER is afflicted by conjunction to Mars but will not participate seriously against him because his periods do not concur with a major progression involving the Ascendant. But in the 3rd House semi-square the Ascendant his education though promising at the start would be lost to him. Mars in the same position against him would cut his schooling short.

URANUS is the most seriously-afflictive planet in the chart because he is in bad aspect to Neptune and Saturn & directing his malevolence against the body because opposition the Ascendant & the Part of Peril there. His age-periods coincide with years that are under severe major progressions. At age 26 in 1934, with progressed Moon conjunct Uranus, square Saturn & opposition Neptune, the Ascendant & Part of Peril, the worst accident of his life befell him, following the pattern we expect by now. He was struck by an automobile, the right side of his head cut open, the bones of a foot & several ribs broken, and rendered unconscious for several days. The concussion was so severe that further education was no longer possible and over the following five years he suffered a complete nervous breakdown. The nature of his injuries is clearly reflected by these malefics, particularly when operating during the disastrous Uranian period.

Since history repeats itself, the progressed Moon will be conjunct Uranus again in September 1961 setting off the same effects as in 1934. His age 53 denotes the Uranian period of disastrous participation in the major progression at that time of Sun 9 Libra opposition Saturn, and Mercury 5 Scorpio opposition Lilith & square the Moon in the injurious 8th House. Our only consolation is that we are forewarned & may be able to appease the aspect or mitigate its effect because we have time to prepare for the eventuality.

* * * * *

CHART FOR A T-SQUARE

9:55:00 a.m. LMT Sept. 23, 1900, 90W12 38N

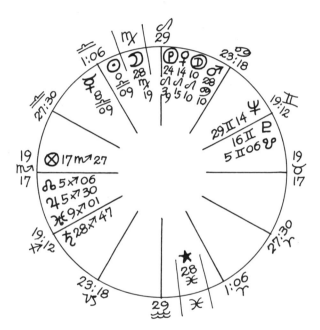

This is the natal chart of a little boy.   He was
born in St. Louis, Missouri, and what befell him can
be verified by the newspapers there for the dates of
September 5, 1914, a month later, and exactly a year
later (September 5, 1915), as presented in the text.

THE T-SQUARE IN YOUR CHART

When the natal chart shows a planet in opposition to another, and each of them square to a planet that is NOT in opposition to anything, the design formed thereby is called a T-square, and the place that is empty stands waiting to be filled (thus "closing the T-square" and timing an event in the person's life).

Many of us with such a configuration are very apprehensive about it and almost always without cause, since the average chart does not present the simultaneous afflictions necessary to result in tragedy: no, the human race is more blessed than that. This usually has to do with balancing something in life by ending a waiting period and going to fulfillment.

In Jacob's chart on the opposite page, Saturn and Neptune in opposition to each other square the Moon who is not in opposition to anything: thus 28 Pisces in the 4th House becomes the empty place waiting to be filled, at which easily-ascertained time an event of importance will take place. We say easily ascertained because it is easy to see that the first conjunction to 28 Pisces will be by the progressed Moon which in the natal ephemeris occurs 14 days after Jacob's birth, signifying 14 years after, or age 14.

Such a chart is first examined for any mitigating influence which may sustain the native in adversity. Benefics angular & unafflicted will do this - or the Part of Fortune not readable as the Part of Misfortune; the Ascendant & its ruler not afflicted, and no part of the T-square in the 8th House. Failing this we progress the chart for the year indicated & again seek a saving grace in the progressed positions that might nullify any disaster -- but even so, we always advise the native to use precautionary safeguards in the progressed critical period, to avert the worst.

In noting the protection given here (by Jupiter & the good node in the 1st House, Fortuna close to the Ascendant, & the ruler Mars trined by the Ascendant) we are nonetheless dismayed by a host of afflictions hardly ever seen in a single chart, so that this T-square must result in tragedy. The protection given was therefore what accounted for living to 14 years.

The Part of Fortune in the 12th House or the 12th Sign Pisces or the Pisces decanate of a watery Sign, as here, becomes the Part of Mis-fortune.   Anything in the same degree as the nodes threatens a casualty (here it is Jupiter, otherwise the Greater Benefic). The Lesser Benefic Venus squares the Ascendant which is exactly conjunct the "cursèd degree of the cursèd Sign" marking the body for misfortune without saving grace from Venus. The always ill-starred 29th degree appears on the Midheaven (Fate), also on the malefic in the death-8th, a party to the T-square.   The 1st cusp plus the ruler of the 8th and then minus Saturn gives the Part of Peril (P) 24:39 Leo. The 1st cusp plus the 8th cusp, then minus the Moon, gives us the Part of Death (D) 10 Leo. We add the arc 14:00, and find that in 14 years the Part of Death will exactly conjunct the Part of Peril & semisquare Mercury, the ruler of the death-8th, threatening a major injury.

Jacob was the youngest of four children, having a sister & two brothers, none of whom ever married, as shown by Saturn ruler brethren-3rd afflicted by Neptune and the domestic Moon. His father was crippled (shown by Saturn ruler father-4th in hip Sign Sagittarius square both Sun & Moon and opposition Neptune the abnormal-&-lame), and he always deferred to the mother's wishes, as revealed by the mother-Moon in a

Sign rising before the one the father-Sun is in and
so taking the lead over him. Jacob had a pet kitten
(Venus rules cats) and we see only the Part of Death
coming between them (Venus & the boy's ruler, Mars).
This kitten proved to be of ultimate importance when
progressed Venus at age 14 moved to 29 Leo, conjunct
the Fate line and sextile Neptune who is the betray-
ing party in the T-square by being in the death-8th.

On September 5, 1914, Jacob disappeared while on
an errand. The progressed Moon 28 Pisces had closed
the T-square & was in 29 Pisces square Neptune while
the progressed Ascendant was in 29 Scorpio, quincunx
Neptune in the death-8th and square the end-of-life-
4th cusp, decreeing death. Note that the 150-degree
quincunx is the natural distance from the 8th to the
Ascendant, therefore it is one of the death aspects.

The progressed Mars 6 Leo conjoined the midpoint
between natal Mars (the boy himself) and Venus ruler
of the 7th (his opponent: another person) bringing a
vibration of danger and assailment. Venus, being in
mutual reception (with the Sun) has exchange status
and can "get out of what he gets into" which was the
case: nothing has ever been learned of the assailant
who got safely away - but he was a killer, as proved
by the Solstice Point of the Part of Death 19 Taurus
conjunct his cusp, the 7th, and semisextile the 8th.
Note also that Venus his ruler is exactly semisquare
Neptune the betrayer in the 8th House. Besides the
Ascendant and the Moon, both Venus the murderer and
Saturn the Reaper had progressed to that ill-starred
and fateful 29th degree aspecting Neptune, signaling
the end of the Signs and the end of the way for him.

A month later, the body of a large man was taken
from a nearby swamp, his hands tied behind him with
his own belt. He had been murdered and thrown into

the water.   Jacob was small for his age, so the family did not identify the body: it was buried and the
search for Jacob continued.   However, the pet kitten
kept following the grieving mother about, crying and
pulling at her skirt, always in the direction of the
doorway, until it occurred to her that the body may
have been Jacob's after all, and she was being led
to it.   The body was exhumed and, the great bloating
having disappeared, it was identified as Jacob's and
buried by the family on September 5, 1915, exactly a
year after his murder.   Two planets ruling the house
of burial, the 4th, may account for the two burials.

We have mentioned the Solstice Point as explained
on page 103 herein.   It is worthwhile to apply this
procedure to the progressed planets as well as natal
planets, and here we see that the progressed Mercury
ruler 8th in 0:31 Scorpio (swamps & stagnant waters)
had its Solstice Point in 29 Aquarius conjunct the
end-of-life-4th, square the progressed Ascendant and
trine Neptune in the 8th.   Good luck deserted Jacob
because the progressed Part of Fortune 1 Sagittarius
had its Solstice Point in 28 Capricorn in opposition
to natal Mars, significator of Jacob himself.   Even
the 8th cusp was inimical, having moved to 1:06 Cancer, its Solstice Point in 28 Gemini opposing Saturn
(opposed to allowing any more Time) and squaring the
Moon (both parties to the T-square), and semisextil-
ing his own significator, Mars, in his fall by Sign.

Let those of us who live in dread of approaching
bad aspects in the chart, especially beginners, look
back to the second paragraph of this chapter and be
of good cheer, because such simultaneous afflictions
are very rare, and a T-square need never cause fear.

✯ ✯ ✯ ✯ ✯

WHO'S THAT KNOCKING AT MY DOOR?

Your home is represented by the 4th House, whose cusp is its doorway & point of entry, its threshold. Leading up to your home is the 3rd House, representing the near neighborhood or locality adjacent to your house; and because any visitor must necessarily be in that near-neighborhood-3rd in order to reach your home, any planet in the 3rd House is representative of the visitor who is "knocking at your door".

There are three ways in which the planet may be there, the first being at birth: a natal planet. It describes the visitors through life who will make a lasting impression on you -- and if it rules the 7th House one of them will set his or her cap for you in the future, object matrimony & whether the proposal is accepted or not. Such a natal planet registers when aspected by progression or by a strong transit, bringing that visitor to your door. With a planet in the 3rd House at birth, you are sure to remember the first who called when you were old enough to notice.

The second way in which the planet may be there is by progression, to describe visitors who may come during the length of time it is in the 3rd, which is approximately three or four years for the Moon; much longer for the others. As they aspect natal planets they bring visitors, and are themselves susceptible to being roused by strong transits into developing their visitor-possibility into visitor-probability.

The third way in which a planet may bring guests is by transit when a planet in the current ephemeris is in your 3rd House. Slow-moving planets make more impressive visits than the faster ones, and register when they aspect either natal or progressed planets.

We can not only tell what sort of visitors are to come but also how they arrive, what their visit and discourse will be like, and whether they are sick or well, masculine or feminine, welcome or not, invited or uninvited, and also their method of leave-taking.

A planet in the 3rd House in the Sign on the 4th denotes a tie-up with the 4th House in a 12th-House way involving apologies, so that the visitor will be asked to excuse the family & the way the place looks just now, or will be cautioned not to trip over anything because the 4th (ruling excavations, mines and wells, etc.) has to do with holes in the ground and irregularities in the floor level - including steps.

If the planet is retrograde, the visitor is backward in some way by arriving later than expected or leaving later than he should. He is usually in ill health & sure to complain about one thing or another although he also has something in mind that he wants to reveal but being retrograde keeps it to himself.

The malefics come without invitation but when not afflicting the Ascendant are not unwelcome. Other planets are usually invited guests and more or less welcome according to their good or bad aspect to the Ascendant. Jupiter, Venus and particularly the Moon may have a special or standing invitation and may be encouraged to come again. The better a malefic is conditioned by Sign and good aspect to a benefic the more likely the caller is to be a perfect gentleman. We are reminded of "The Young Visiters", an amusing book ostensibly written by an anonymous little girl, according to J. M. Barrie, whose hero was described as "a gentleman, not quite but very nearly" which is apropos of a malefic well-placed by Sign but in a weakly bad aspect to Jupiter or Venus, the significators of courtesy, politeness and good breeding.

The Moon & Venus represent feminine callers, the others masculine (although Mercury being convertible may represent either sex: perhaps according to that of the Sign he is in). Neptune is considered to be the higher octave of Venus and thereby feminine, although named for the masculine god of the sea. This is quite consistent for so contradictory a planet as Neptune who can be bewildered, befogged and bemused.

The SUN is an early caller, stays all day and may return next day, making himself right at home, & accepting service graciously, discoursing well on matters of benefit to all. He is a welcome guest and in good health unless afflicted by malefics; a well-set and rather pretentious and superior person, arriving by vehicle and taking his time about leaving: you do not shut the door on him, but watch him go, smiling.

The MOON never comes twice at the same hour, but fits easily into the circle as one of the family and helps with the dishes, talks about everyday, popular or domestic affairs, and agrees quickly with others. If afflicted, she is physically or emotionally upset and if in any aspect at all with Mars she raises the subject of an operation. She is a welcome guest and one who needs no invitation, arrives in an unpretentious conveyance and leaves very quietly and without haste, remembering to take a souvenir home with her.

SATURN is an uninvited guest who arrives without warning and almost stealthily, overstays his welcome and drags out his leave-taking. His speech is serious, sometimes boresome, critical and recriminatory, and his voice becomes querulous. If retrograde, he suffers from an illness that will become chronic and he is conscious of having poor teeth and bad fingernails. He is apt to become a problem person in time. He likes to walk & usually arrives & leaves on foot.

MARS is also an uninvited guest, arriving noisily and boisterously: may jump the fence, slam the door, or slap his host playfully: he seldom stays long and is too active to sit still or stay on the subject, & if retrograde has an illness that will become acute; he perspires easily, bears a scar or mark, and has a voice heard through the house. He is likely to talk about subjects not usually mentioned, may be bold or rude; contradicts, disagrees & interrupts, and is so self-assured that he makes your decisions for you or directs the conversation his way. He takes his leave soon, marching away with a jaunty & debonair salute.

MERCURY makes short, stop-over calls, and usually drops in without invitation while en route elsewhere and may have notified you of such intention in order to deliver a message, document, etc. He is often a coming-&-going guest, restless, too nervous to over-stay his welcome; and his discourse touches lightly on a diversity of subjects. If retrograde he lisps, hesitates in speech, or repeats himself; and if also in bad aspect to Saturn or Uranus he is in danger of a serious breakdown. He gesticulates a great deal, waving on arrival and also in speeding away on foot.

VENUS is a good-looking, friendly & welcome guest making a social call, bringing a present, discours-ing pleasantly, speaking well of all, usually paying you a compliment, and praising everything. She has poise and good manners; strokes the cat or dog, pats the children on the head, thanks you prettily when served refreshments, & may kiss you on arriving and when leaving. If retrograde, the visitor may be too plump, use pomade or perfume that "rocks the room" & may appear to be over-dressed or else rather untidy.

JUPITER is a jovial, heavier-set visitor, invited & welcome, arriving in a conveyance and soon finding

the most comfortable chair.   He is given to sitting
with folded hands & discoursing agreeably on topics
related to charity, religion, philosophy, travel and
sports or parades; rarely interrupts others but ends
by pointing a moral. He eats very heartily & enjoys
his glass of wine, pats his stomach & never fails to
smack his lips over a good meal.   If retrograde, he
is overweight, and if in bad aspect to the Ascendant
his visit costs you money. He leaves in genial mood
bestowing his blessing - with you urging him to come
again soon.   He seems to give you hope and comfort.

URANUS is uninvited, showing up unexpectedly, to
disrupt the routine and upset other plans, and if in
bad aspect to the Ascendant is unwelcome.   His discourse is scientific, political, universal in scope,
with a new slant on ordinary topics, spontaneous and
unrehearsed.   If conjunct, trine or parallel Venus,
a mutual attraction or even love at first sight is a
possibility; his other aspects to Venus also denote
romantic interest, not necessarily platonic.   He is
unmarried at the moment. His departure is abrupt, &
leaves you feeling once more free of his domination.

NEPTUNE makes surprise calls without invitation &
secret visits, and may use the back door in arriving
or leaving -- and when he finally goes is indecisive
about it and then just fades away. His discourse is
vague, about peculiar, sensational or hearsay topics
and he enjoins you to secrecy and may veer away from
the strict truth, being generally uninformed or misinformed. If retrograde, he is ill or disfigured in
some way & wears glasses. He often requests a gift.

Two or more planets in the 3rd denote two or more
visitors arriving at the same time, together or not.
If transits, they are complete outsiders calling for
a contribution, asking directions or favors & so on.

* * * * *

A CHART FOR DECISION POINTS

10;25;30 p.m. EST Dec. 2, 1914 - 73W57 40N45

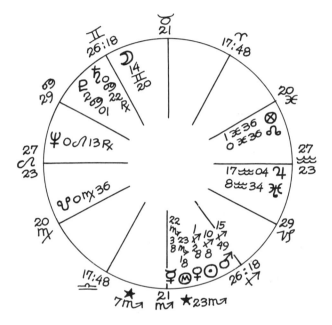

This natal chart for a woman shows that although the Sun, Moon, Mars, Venus and ruler of Ascendant in adaptable Common Signs signify great adaptability to life, Mercury in a Fixed Sign denotes great firmness of mind, so that she makes her own decisions regardless of advice. Some of these are not calculated to operate to her advantage, however, since Mercury is square good-judgment-Jupiter and also the Ascendant.

THE DECISIONS THAT YOU WILL MAKE

The planet of decisions is Mercury, ruler of the mental processes and possessor of the ability to go this way or that according to where the pressure is greatest. That is because he rules mercury or quick-silver, the liquid metal capable of going in any direction, quickly susceptible to persuasion, and like mercurial people themselves, whose decisions depend as much on outer influence as on inner conviction. Now, how are we to put this knowledge to workable use in prefiguring decisions from one's natal chart?

It usually happens that during the 95 days before birth and the 95 days after birth, Mercury "decides" to turn in direction, either retrograde or direct. The Sign-&-degree he is in at turning gives you what this writer calls a Permanent Decision Point, to set down outside the original chart, identifying it by a small star: it is active whenever aspected. Whether Mercury turns before or after birth, the decisions always register during the 95 years after birth. It often happens that the early life registers an event dependent upon a decision made by someone else, more particularly in very early years, as when a parent's decision motivates a child's participation - such as having to accompany the family in changing address.

In the chart on the opposite page, pre-natal Mercury went direct in 7 Scorpio (a Permanent Decision Point) 15 days before birth, denoting 15 years after birth or the period between December 1929 & December 1930. Just the fact that he turned at all would denote a change involving a decision because he is the planet Mercury. He was then in the NEAR-neighborhood 3rd and he squared Uranus in the 6th of ANOTHER neighborhood. Uranus disrupts foundations, thus in

January 1930 the native - by the family's decision -
removed to another neighborhood, miles away.   Note
the Decision Point 7 Scorpio shown outside the 3rd.

Always give continued importance to the planet a
decision point first aspects. Uranus here rules the
marriage-7th, therefore we show the Part of Marriage
(the Ascendant plus the 7th, then minus Venus) which
is (M) 23:18 Scorpio here, conjunct Mercury, so that
she would marry by her own decision. In June 1938,
by age-arc 23:30 her converse Venus in 7 Scorpio was
conjunct the Point and square Uranus-ruler-7th & she
decided to marry - although Venus detrimented showed
that her heart was not in it: it was an unwise move.

Another Decision Point to note is 23 Scorpio conjunct Mercury and the Part of Marriage, marking the
place where her pre-natal Mercury turned retrograde
35 days before birth denoting 35 years after, or the
period between December 1949 and December 1950. His
first turn was direct and she went forward, but this
was retrograde and she reversed, so to speak. Since
her pre-natal Uranus was then 7 Aquarius and square
the original Point she decided on a disruptive move,
a divorce, in March 1950.   Always notice the planet
accompanying the one that turns if it makes aspects,
giving you a clue according to the planet & aspect.

Directing the planets at the rate of a degree for
a year, note that Jupiter who rules her 5th of love-
interests reached 22 Pisces at the age arc 35/36 and
trined Mercury conjunct the Part of Marriage and she
became engaged. The next year (1951) she married as
Jupiter reached 23 Pisces and trined (M) 23 Scorpio.

At the same rate of a degree for a year we direct
these Points to conjunct or oppose natal planets. In
1947/48 the age arc 33/34 moved the Point 7 Scorpio

to 10 Sagittarius conjunct the Sun which is always a
gain, especially in the home-4th. Her pre-natal Sun
was 7 Scorpio conjunct the Decision Point, while her
pre-natal Mercury in 21 Scorpio was conjunct the 4th
cusp, so of course she bought a home that year. Why
do we say bought instead of inherited, which is also
a 4th-House possibility? Because Mercury rules her
money-2nd and was going into her home-4th, therefore
that was where her money was going. The Moon & Mars
are opposition at birth, signifying a cutting-off or
separative kind of operation. Five years after buy-
ing the house & at age arc 38/39, the directed Point
was 15 Sagittarius conjunct Mars-opposition-Moon and
she sold the house (Mars-4th) cutting her ownership.

In 1958/59 the age arc 44/45 took Uranus to 22 of
Pisces trine Mercury in the home-4th, and also took
Jupiter to 1 Aries trine Venus in the 4th. Whenever
Uranus and Jupiter trine anything what they bring is
in the nature of a windfall and by gift, and as Jupiter rules her legacy 8th it would come by a death.
Since Uranus then trined Mercury-ruler-money-2nd and
Jupiter trined Venus-of-money she received the money
to buy and furnish another home for herself in 1960,
given by her mother one month after the death of her
father in January. He had left everything solely to
the mother whose decision it was to invest a sum in
that way. We note again that the original Decision
Point 7 Scorpio timed a move decided by the parents,
and in this instance the age arc 44/45 directed that
Point to 21 Sagittarius exactly semisextile the cusp
of the home-4th: a home by somebody else's decision.
By Secondary Progression Venus, ruler mother-10th in
10 Sagittarius, came conjunct the Sun in the 4th, as
confirmation of gain in the home through the mother.

☆ ☆ ☆ ☆ ☆

NATAL CHART FOR A SUICIDE

8:00:00 a.m. EST July 25, 1917 – 81W40 41N30

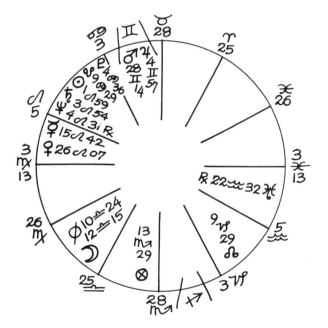

    This is the chart of a woman who could easily en-
tertain the thought of suicide, because her ruler is
Mercury-of-thought in the suicide-12th House, square
Fortuna in Scorpio; and the Sun conjuncts Neptune of
suicide, who rules her "manner of death" 8th House.

TO WARN OR NOT TO WARN

There is a diversity of opinion among astrologers as to whether a person should be told of future disaster threatening in his natal chart.　Many believe in free will, holding that being forewarned is being forearmed: some are fatalistic and see no possible evading of the catastrophe, so that it would be only a disservice to worry the person pointlessly: others feel that the knowledge might condition him toward attracting or even precipitating his own disaster, like Job, who cried that the thing he greatly feared had THEREFORE come upon him.　This is undeniably a moot point worthy of our deep concern in his behalf.

In the natal chart on the opposite page, we find the Midheaven ill-starred by conjunction to the malefic Pleiades - the so-called "Weeping Sisters" - so that her Fate and other 10th-House affairs would be something to weep about: particularly since the Midheaven is further singled out for attention by exact conjunction to the Sun's Solstice Point in 28 Taurus (see page 103).　Any angle or planet thus emphasized must be reckoned with in timing events because it is empowered by the Sun & thus has conferred authority to act.　In this chart, the Sun rules the 12th House (weeping) and the ruler of the Ascendant is there in bad aspect to the Part of Fortune which, when in Pisces or a Pisces decanate is the Part of Misfortune.

As the Midheaven moves forward at the Sun's rate 0:59' per year and passes over Jupiter & Mars in the 10th House, we still do not expect disaster, because these two are intercepted or held in abeyance & also are not afflicted by bad planetary aspect at birth. But coming to Pluto **is** a bad omen because he rules the end-of-life-4th House and is eight houses after

the 4th and is conjunct the midpoint between the two
rulers of this 8th, Jupiter and Neptune, waiting for
a major progressed aspect to "alert" them. This the
Midheaven does in 36-degrees 36-minutes which is the
Solar Arc equivalent of 37 years, disclosing her age
at the time for warning -- falling in the year 1954.

If this were all, her warning might comprise only
simple advice to be ready for an emergency (ruled by
the 11th House where we find Pluto). But if there is
additional testimony of trouble that year - the more
so if there is further emphasis on the rulers of the
8th of danger - some calamity is foreshadowed.   We
require at least three confirming major progressed
aspects before a dire warning is justified.   These,
unhappily, were all present in her chart as follows:

By adding the arc 36:36 to Mars' place we see him
in 4:50 Leo conjunct Neptune a ruler of the 8th: the
other ruler Jupiter moves to 11:33 Cancer square the
midpoint between the Moon and Lilith-of-poisoning.
The Moon in 18:51 Scorpio is conjunct the Cursèd Degree (page 30, Alan Leo's Degrees of the Zodiac) and
sesquare Pluto, a contributory-to-death aspect. The
Ascendant-ruler Mercury in 22:18 Virgo is quincunx
Uranus (and on the day of the event itself the Minor
Moon in 22:29 Aquarius was exactly conjunct Uranus).

As Mars left his interception in the employment-
10th & also got through Cancer the Sign of his fall,
the native's former bad luck waned & as he came conjunct the Sun in the 11th (circumstances) & powerful
in Leo, her circumstances brightened & she obtained
a good job in Las Vegas, Nevada.   But as he left the
Sun the following year and came to Saturn whose hold
is weaker in the Sign of his detriment, she lost one
job after another.   During the final 30 minutes (six
months of Mars' transit) she was without any income,

entirely dependent on a roommate, so that a complete estrangement developed between them: something to be expected under Mars' forthcoming conjunction to Neptune, the planet of alienation, snubs and ostracism.

We may remark here that the student should always forecast a long period of tribulation when the natal Mars-of-trouble is due to conjunct several malefics by progression when they are concentrated in the map rather than dispersed around the chart (where he can not so easily form the conjunction-aspect). Telling the person this will encourage him to "stick it out" because if he cannot anticipate better times ahead he may lose heart entirely and let Mars win, instead of realizing that he is only forcing a way through.

She became abnormally bewildered and nervous as Mars met Neptune & matters approached the crisis to be counted on when Mars transits any malefic by progression. This is also true of any exact bad aspect to the Nodes or to any planet in a critical degree - and as the arc 36:36 moved the Ascendant to 9 Libra squaring the Nodes & exactly sesquaring Uranus, and Mars completed his conjunction to Neptune on October 4th, 1954, she took an overdose of sleeping-pills.

Neptune rules drugs, narcotics, anything that induces comatose conditions, suspended animation, etc. as well as suicide. She went into a coma which was unbroken (Fixed Sign Leo) until her death five days later at 9:10 a.m. PST Oct. 9, 1954 at 115W08 36N10.

The question here is therefore: would warning her have been a saving grace or an added discouragement, seeing that the Fate-line, the Midheaven, was now in 4 Cancer conjunct Pluto and semisextile both Neptune and the progressed Mars, and the emotional Moon progressed to conjunct the cursèd degree in 19 Scorpio?

Whenever we see a malefic whose forward motion is going to take him over another malefic, whatever the method of progression used, be sure that it is going to register at that time in the person's life. Even if there is nothing else afflicting the chart we may expect a period of stress at least and it seems only logical to prepare for whatever is denoted - such as insurance if the 2nd-of-possessions or 4th-of-residence is under threat; or a savings-account to handle possible heavy expenses; or medical & dental examinations if the 6th is the one receiving the impact.

The Part of Fortune should always be considered in charts of this nature. If in the 12th House, the 12th Sign Pisces or a Pisces decanate as here, or in bad aspect with Neptune (natural ruler of Pisces and the 12th House) it is usually the Part of Misfortune to some extent, if only in the matters ruled by the house it is in. In this chart, Mercury-of-Logic is square to the Part of Fortune in Fixed Signs so that probably no amount of reasoning could have moved her & especially with Fortuna's dispositor Mars exactly sesquare from Gemini, the reasoning-or-unreasoning.

It is often possible with advance information of impending trouble to do something intentionally that is allied in a harmonious way with whatever is indicated and thus APPEASE the aspect. If sickness is forecast, take some simple medicine, not a drug. If the 7th House is afflicted, suggesting trouble with a partner in particular, take a separation of a non-committal kind, a vacation apart with no definite break decided on or even considered while the transit continues. This appeases the aspect, because a separation of sorts has occurred without commitment.

When any crisis is denoted however, always advise the person not to be alone; stay with a friend of an

optimistic and encouraging turn of mind, or seek out
an understanding relative or minister when the going
is hard. Even though a non-escapable calamity comes
to pass, their aid & comfort can ease the situation.

If there is a mutual reception in the natal chart
(two planets, each in the other's natural Sign) such
give-and-take enables the native to change places at
will or get out of what he got into: which will help
you to give a truthful and more encouraging forecast
on occasion.   Encouragement is reassuring to those
born in the Sign Leo in particular because they have
that childlike attitude of trust-or-all-is-lost, but
this native with Venus in Leo (a loving heart) could
not ask for anything because Mercury is in the house
of denial and opposition Uranus in the house of aid,
and she could not get out of what she got into since
there is no mutual reception in her chart to assist.

Everything considered, would you have warned her?

* * * * *

Venus in Leo

When Venus is in Leo
The heart with love is filled.
But in the silent 12th House
The words of love are stilled.
The words that she would fain receive
And would delight confiding,
Excepting that she has no leave,
And so they stay in hiding.

✯ ✯ ✯ ✯ ✯

NATAL CHART FOR HARRY S. TRUMAN

4:14:00 p.m. LMT May 8, 1884 - 94W15 37N30

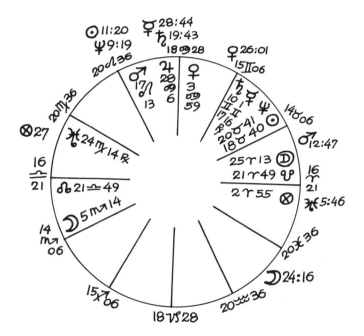

Example:

29:60 whole Sign
Venus -3:59 Cancer
Solstice Point Venus 26:01 Gemini (on Cancer line)

THE SOLSTICE POINTS IN YOUR CHART

Surely the easiest point to figure in your natal chart, helping you to time many events in your life, is the "antiscia" or Solstice Point of each planet. They mark a TURNING POINT in some way when aspected.

The solstice itself is the Sun's turning point in 0-Cancer and 0-Capricorn as he goes back to the celestial equator from his greatest distance away: they designate the Summer Solstice on June 21st and the Winter Solstice on December 21st each year.

A planet's Solstice POINT is its distance from 0-Cancer or 0-Capricorn -- whichever it is nearer -- carried over to the other side of the solstice used, but we offer here a quicker & surer way of doing it. Take the planet's REMAINING degrees-&-minutes in the Sign it is in for the degrees-&-minutes for its Solstice Point. The Sign to use is the one on the same line with the planet's, in the following diagram:

Capricorn	:	Sagittarius
Aquarius	:	Scorpio
Pisces	:	Libra
Aries	:	Virgo
Taurus	:	Leo
Gemini	:	Cancer

Note the calculation of Venus' Solstice Point on the opposite page, & how we show all of them outside the wheel. A progression or heavy transit aspecting

a Solstice Point activates the planet it belongs to,
& any aspect that planet made natally & any that the
Solstice Point itself made to a planet in the chart.

Progress the Solstice Point at the Sun's rate of
a degree for a year and note any aspects it forms to
the natal planets and angles, observing particularly
any action of the Ascendant-ruler's Solstice Point.

In Mr. Truman's life - whose chart we are using -
each time his Ascendant-ruler Venus or her Solstice
Point makes or receives an aspect he can expect some
development of personal importance. In 1886, age 2,
Venus' S. Pt in 28 Gemini aspected Jupiter ruler 3rd
and his brother was born. In 1889, age 5, it was in
1 Cancer aspecting Mercury natural ruler 3rd, at the
birth of his sister. Not until it reached 3:59 Cancer in 1892 to conjunct Venus herself in the school-
9th did he start school (age 8). At age 40 in 1924,
the progressed Sun in 26 Gemini conjoined the S. Pt.
at the birth of his daughter (note that this Sun is
ruler of the 11th (child of the marriage-7th): Uranus ruler children-5th has his Solstice Point 5 Aries
and the progressed Moon came to its conjunction).

In 1954, age 70, when the progressed Ascendant in
26 Sagittarius exactly opposed Venus' Solstice Point
he was operated on for appendicitis. He might have
died because progressed Venus who also rules his 8th
of death was 16:21 Cancer square the Ascendant - and
Mars natural ruler of the 8th House was 23:44 Virgo,
conjunct disorganizing-Uranus in the hospital-12th.
How often we forget that the 8th House rules surgery
as well as death, since surgical removal of any part
of the body means death to that part principally and
not necessarily the end of life itself. The Moon is
Giver-of-Life here and was exactly conjunct the Sun,
giving healthy functioning of the constitution then,

even though a part of him did die by surgery because
the progressed Sun in 25 Cancer squared the Part of
Deaths (D) 25:13 Aries.   (For (D), see page 150.)

The Part of Deaths was always activated by deaths
in his circle.   In 1909, age-arc 25, it moved to 20
Taurus exactly conjunct Neptune at the death of his
grandmother, while Venus' S. Pt 21 Cancer was square
the nodes. In 1914, age 30, his father passed on as
the Moon's S. Pt 24:46 Pisces aspected (D), and also
Venus' S. Pt and the natal Uranus. In 1945, age 61,
while he was Vice-President, the Part of Death moved
from his partner-7th House to 26 Gemini conjunct the
S. Pt of Venus as the death of his partner President
Roosevelt affected him very personally. In 1947, at
age 63, his mother passed away. The progressed Part
of Death reached 28 Gemini and the Moon's S. Pt came
to 28 Aries, both exactly aspecting Jupiter (and the
Solstice Point of Mercury) in the mother-10th House:
Jupiter's S. Pt 5 Leo now squared the Moon herself.

His political career began in earnest in 1922, as
progressed Venus came exactly conjunct Jupiter & the
S. Pt of Mercury in the 10th House at age 38 when he
was appointed judge. In 1935 at 51, Venus' S. Pt in
17 Leo came conjunct Mars in the career-10th, and he
was appointed Congressman. In 1940 at 56, he became
Senator when progressed Venus in the 10th House came
to the sextile of Uranus: Fortuna moved to 28 Taurus
sextile Jupiter (and Mercury's S. Pt) in the 10th.

In 1944 at 60, he became Vice-President under orb
of tremendous oncoming aspects not exact for another
year - therefore it was a lesser position due to become greater. 1945, age 61, was his Full Moon year,
the progressed Moon 16 Capricorn & the Sun 16 Cancer
bringing fulfillment through a death, as the Part of
Death came to Venus' S. Pt exactly. Jupiter's S. Pt

was in 2:54 Leo trine the Part of Fortune; the S. Pt
of the Moon ruler 10th in 16 Aries exactly conjoined
the public service 7th, and Mars (in the career-10th
at birth) was in 18 Virgo exactly trine the Sun and
sextile the Midheaven, and that year he succeeded to
the Presidency - a most Jupiterian position in life.

His career attained this fulfillment by irregular
procedure, as it were, due to the death in office of
the President rather than by regular election. This
is revealed by progressed Jupiter in 9 Leo & exactly
conjunct the Solstice Point of Neptune -- the planet
that is always significant of irregular procedure.

From all this we see that there can be no disput-
ing the importance of the Solstice Points as well as
their accuracy in pinpointing events in the life.
In addition, the solstice points being fixed, we can
use them in rectifying the time of birth, insofar as
progressed aspects between them and the Midheaven or
Ascendant are exact or not, in timing the events.

Looking ahead therefore to 1956/1957, age 72, the
progressed Sun in 28 Cancer conjuncts Jupiter & also
the Solstice Point of Mercury and sextiles Fortuna's
Solstice Point, while progressed Jupiter 11 Leo conjuncts the Sun's Solstice Point. All of this brings
him increased prominence, happiness and gain in this
period, especially around April 1957 when progressed
Moon in 3:59 Cancer is exactly conjunct Venus in the
9th House, conferring formal honors on him, bringing
travel, foreign interests, publications and, best of
all, grandchildren, who are also ruled by the 9th.

(Written in September 1956, published in A.F.A. Bulletin January 1957 before the grandchild's birth-ex-
pectation was made public on February 15th, 1957)

✴ ✴ ✴ ✴ ✴

THE MARRIAGE SUN

The two parties to a marriage are individuals and therefore represented by the Sun (the ego) in their charts; so that as both persons have progressed to a point of marriage so have their Suns become one. To find what this writer originated and calls the Marriage Sun (M-S) simply add the age to the natal Sun in each chart, then add the directed Suns together.

In this example, he was born on June 21, 1901 and she on May 21, 1902: they married in November, 1920.

```
                                   S dg mn
She 19 - Directed Sun        2 19:11
He  20 - Directed Sun  /     3 19:16
The Marriage Sun    Libra (6) 8:27
```

Since marriage is a feminine institution, we will read the M-S in her chart, with the 10th 27 Scorpio; 11th, 21 Sagittarius; 12th, 14 Capricorn; Ascendant, 12:31 Aquarius; 2nd, 24 Pisces; and 3rd in 0 Taurus.

In 1928 their divorce was granted when the M-S in 15 Libra opposed Venus, but they were reconciled the following year when the M-S trined Jupiter 16 Aquarius. In 1931 the M-S trined Pluto 18 Gemini, ruler legalizing-9th in the domestic-4th when they adopted a baby girl; the adoption became final in 1933 when the M-S 20 Scorpio sextiled Uranus in the adoption-11th House. They separated when the M-S was square Saturn in 27 Capricorn, but were reconciled in 1942, drawn by the trine to Neptune 0 Cancer in the child-5th. In 1943 they separated when the M-S 0 Scorpio was quincunx the Sun 0 Gemini, ruler of marital-7th, and were divorced in 1945, the decree becoming final when the M-S 3 Scorpio was conjunct the North Node & exactly sesquare Pluto. (He then married another.)

☆ ☆ ☆ ☆ ☆

A CHART FOR FILING A DOCUMENT

10:30:00 a.m. PST April 13, 1951, 118W15 34N

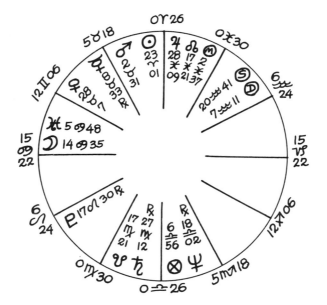

MOON (♂ ♅) ⚹ ♀ - □ ♆ - □ ☉ - ⚹ ♄ - △ ♃ - ⚹ ♀

✴ ✴ ✴ ✴ ✴

YOUR RECORDED DOCUMENTS
HAVE ASTROLOGICAL VALUE

Some of us have no dependable birth data, in some
instances not even the date itself, so reliance must
be placed on horary charts because they give a picture of surrounding conditions both before and after
asking the question; and also on certain charts set
for the time of filing important documents.   These
latter charts can be progressed & read for the owner
as long as they remain his property because they are
thus personally identified with him in a mundane way
(that is, regarding outside, worldly affairs such as
the houses rule, and particularly the matter related
to the house which concerns the document itself).

Even though you do have an authentic natal chart,
document-charts are very illuminating in reading the
future developments in other houses for yourself, in
the same manner as for those who use them in lieu of
the natal chart they lack.

Set the chart for the time stamped on the record-
ed document, which usually appears in both hours and
minutes as it did on the "Notice of Completion" document covering the building of a home represented by
the chart on the opposite page and which is the sole
property of the woman represented by the 1st House &
intended for her personal use. As usual, Mercury is
the document itself and the 4th House designates the
property (whose resale value is shown by the 10th).

It is evident that the property is owned outright
free and clear, as shown by the rulers of the 1st &
4th in their own Signs; the Sun ruler possession-2nd
exalted and elevated, and the Part of Fortune in the
4th.   Cancer rising often discloses that the person
owns real estate now or is planning toward that end.

The Property

First of all, you want to know what your property is like, its value & the neighborhood value; what is to happen on the grounds as time goes on, & how long you will retain the property or keep the document in your own name entirely (or have a trust deed on it).

Venus ruler of the property-4th is in Taurus, the Sign of loam that is good & productive of both fruit and flowers. Her sextile to Jupiter provides fruit-trees and vines; her trine to Saturn in Virgo gives vegetables. All of these were present in abundance, this being part of a countryside-acre in California.

The Part of Fortune IMPROVES any department where found. In the 4th it shows cultivation (Libra) that increases the land value (ruler Venus in Taurus) and attention that increases the value of the house. In the 4th House, Neptune "idealizes" the design of the dwelling, its furnishings and color scheme, and also the landscaping. Being retrograde, the fishpond and waterlilies would come later, but from the first the desire for seclusion ruled by Neptune in the 4th and the within-limits characteristic of Saturn-conjunct-the-4th account for entirely enclosing the property with a high wire fence. It would be decorative and wreathed in roses because Venus-of-beauty rules this property-4th, and Neptune veils, rather than hides.

Saturn in or conjunct the 4th in any chart builds up an estate of greater value; while the Sun, ruling the possession-2nd, increases the worth appreciably and resale value thereby when exalted & in the 10th, which is the value price of the property-4th - & the more so here since he conjoins the midpoint between Jupiter and Venus the two significators of increase, so that all three benefics are joined in this way.

Saturn in the 3rd describes the near neighborhood
as being older, well-established, very quiet and se-
date in Virgo, with many old and invalid persons because he is retrograde.   These live in an adjoining
religious settlement for retired missionaries - good
& quiet neighbors, keeping their 5 acres of cottages
in good condition as shown by Venus trine to Saturn.
The neighboring couple on the other side are similar
in that they also are good, quiet neighbors, middle-
aged and not too well, but keeping their property in
excellent condition. Venus trine Saturn is friendly.

The Moon having already squared Mars in the 10th,
(cuts) has already cut the asking price of the land.
The ruler of the seller-7th, Saturn, is retrograde &
thus willing to back down; he and the buyer-Moon are
in mutual application to their sextile & well placed
by Sign, signifying friendliness and satisfaction in
closing the deal for less. Harmony is further shown
by all planets either well placed by Sign or dispos-
ited by the benefics, Jupiter, Venus or the Sun,
which also brings peace and protection to the owner.

It is interesting to note that the furnishings of
this house would be highly prized, beautiful & valuable, since the Sun ruler possessions-2nd is high in
the chart, exalted by Sign, and exactly conjunct the
midpoint between Venus ruler home-4th & Jupiter ruler foreign-import-9th, joining value to value in the
form of personal possessions. Perhaps the most outstanding of these is the white marble fireplace dat-
ing back a century and brought from Paris.   Neptune
in the 4th brings enchantment to the home and as co-
ruler of the foreign-9th, a certain Old World grace.
Venus-of-beauty glorifies stone to marble when trine
Saturn-of-granite, thus combining beauty & utility.
All of these points are indicative of valuable property in an excellent neighborhood & due to increase.

Neptune in the 4th can cause chaos on the grounds
when squared by the Moon, as here, but the upheavals
or abnormal conditions have improvement as their aim
because Fortuna is there in orb of trine from Venus,
ruler of the 4th.   Thus there was an extensive flood
control project (definitely ruled by Neptune) as the
Moon progressed through the neighborhood-3rd in 1956
parallel Neptune in the 4th in the public-works Sign
Libra.   The whole frontage was excavated its entire
length, the moat being 25 feet wide and 25 feet deep
with a temporary bridge allowing automobile passage.
The 4th was then 5 Libra squaring disruptive-Uranus,
and these chaotic conditions lasted several months.

Term of ownership

To see how long the document is to remain in this
woman's possession, we must turn to document-Mercury
because all papers of whatever nature come under his
rulership.   Accordingly, we look forward in the 1951
ephemeris for the number of days required for him to
either change Signs or turn in direction - whichever
happens first.   In that number of years the document
undergoes a change - either complete or in a detail.

The observant student may wonder about the length
of time any property may be owned by any one person,
considering that sooner or later Mercury must change
Signs and terminate ownership, and he is the fastest
of the eight planets.   His tenure is generally short
but he can nonetheless stay in a Sign for a very extended period: as witness his position in Virgo from
July 27th, 1951 to October 2nd, measuring 67 days or
67 years' ownership before relinquishing a document.

A change of Signs always means a change of ownership: this may transpire because of an outright sale

or gift or when paid up - or cessation due to death.
It signifies that he is no longer personally identified with the document because it passes to somebody
else and its effects also pass with it; what happens
on the grounds no longer affects the previous owner.

If Mercury turns retrograde it means indirect action and a paper taken back; ownership is incomplete
because of a mortgage or community-property development involving two persons, continuing until Mercury
changes Signs. If he turns direct, it means direct-
action towards putting the property up for sale, and
possibility of selling earlier if he is late in that
Sign and therefore due to leave it sooner. However,
in either case the previous owner continues to be in
the picture and identified with what happens on the
premises until Mercury changes Signs & thereby frees
him from further relationship or obligation there.

In this example, Mercury's first change is not in
direction, since he remains retrograde in the ephemeris until after he changes Signs by backward motion
on April 30, 1951 when in 0 Taurus which is the same
as 30 Aries, a change of Signs. This measures to 17
days in the ephemeris, or 17 years after filing the
document, or 1968 for a major change of ownership.

Confirmation by progressions

The progressions on that date concur very accept-
ably.   Venus-ruler-4th in 18 Gemini trines Neptune;
the Moon-ruler-Ascendant parallels the Sun-ruler-2nd
and trines the Ascendant from the 9th, bringing gain
from a stranger; the Sun conjoining Mercury throws a
new-reading light on the document; and Mars in 14:48
Taurus sextiles the Moon's position on the Ascendant
bringing an opportunity to change, while the 4th itself conjoins Neptune in the 4th, denoting a change.

The best time for filing

If you are electing a good date on which to rec-
ord a document having to do with real estate, choose
a time for filing with Saturn in or conjunct the 4th
cusp so as to increase the land value and be sure of
building up an estate for yourself, which Saturn has
the power to do here. Note that those natives lucky
enough to be born with this configuration will build
up an estate for themselves and often for posterity.

A personal reading

To see how well an important document-chart takes
the place of a non-existent natal chart, this one is
reliably noteworthy. The owner is a middle-aged and
very active woman (Moon-ruler-1st mid-Sign, cardinal
and angular), mainly interested in her family and in
domesticity in general and real estate in particular
(Cancer rising), a well-balanced person (middle decanate) hard to swerve from a course she believes in,
as shown by the Ascendant & ruler fixed by decanate.

Her husband is of foreign birth (ruler 7th in its
foreign-9th) and the marriage is very harmonious, as
shown by the Moon & Saturn, rulers of the 1st & 7th,
in mutual application to the harmony-sextile aspect.

To show the marriages, illnesses & deaths to take
place in this circle, we enter the Part of Marriage,
(M) 2:37 Pisces, Part of Sickness (S) 20:41 Aquarius
and the Part of Deaths (D) 7:11 Aquarius (page 150).

Marriages

Since Mars ruler 5th-of-children exactly sextiles

the Part of Marriage we expect a child to marry this
same year. Six months later, on October 30th with a
New Moon exactly conjunct the 5th cusp trine Uranus-
the-unexpected, the woman's daughter eloped. We see
the elopement planet Neptune in the daughter's 12th-
of-secret-plans, the retrograde condition accounting
for the six months' delay after filing the document.

In 1957, six years after filing the document, the
granddaughter eloped. The Sun had moved to 28 Aries
exactly conjunct the midpoint between marriage-Venus
and Jupiter (ruler grandchild-9th), and the Moon was
exactly conjunct Saturn in the 3rd (which is the 7th
of marriage for the grandchild-9th); he was 17 years
older than she. The Part of Marriage progressed to
8 Pisces in the 9th & sextiled Mercury who rules the
grandchild's marriage-7th - but it was exactly semisquare the Sun, a bad omen, and the marriage ended
in divorce in 1959 when Mars came conjunct Mercury.

Illnesses

Retrograde planets usually represent people whose
health is failing but who will hold back awhile from
death.   Here, Mercury ruler brother-3rd, and Saturn
ruler husband-7th are retrograde, as well as Neptune
co-ruler of the brother-in-law-9th. When progressed
Moon opposed Mercury early in 1960 a brother became
ill & later that year he underwent an operation when
the progressed Mars (surgeon) was conjunct Mercury.

The progressed (S) 0 Pisces exactly opposed the
brother-3rd cusp accounting for his illness; it also
conjoined the brother-in-law-9th & exactly sesquared
the husband-7th, accounting for the serious turn for
the worse in the physical condition of these two men
who were brothers - and who had both been long ill.

Deaths

The planet the Moon last passed over must always
be noted and the difference in their degrees figured
without regard for their actual distance by Signs or
aspect. Here, she last passed over Uranus, the difference between 14:35 and 5:48 being 8-dg 47-min, or
plus-8 months ago (Moon both cardinal & cadent means
months). Since Uranus rules the death-8th and is in
the family Sign Cancer square to the Part of Fortune
(denoting mis-fortune in the family-4th) we say that
a death in the family occurred eight months earlier;
it was the death of her father on August 8th, 1950.

In any natal, horary, mundane or event chart such
as this, with the Moon and ruler of the 8th in major
aspect, Death continues to register in the circle.
The Part of Death is in the house of death, and when
the 8th cusp came to its conjunction the next year &
the Moon came to the parallel of the instantaneous
power Uranus, ruler of the 8th, an accident brought
instantaneous death in traffic to a woman friend.

We will digress at this point to observe that the
rule holds true in natal charts also, where the Moon
last passed over the death-dealing ruler of the 8th.
We not only use the forward-moving Moon after birth,
but the backward-moving Moon before birth as well, &
call it the Converse Moon.   The same number of days
either before or after birth points to the same number of years after birth when the progressed or converse Moon conjuncts or afflicts any natal planet.

It should be remembered that the Part of Death is
never applied to the native, querent or owner of the
document as the case may be, so that no apprehension
need be felt when, as in this case, the ruler of the
Ascendant is conjunct the Part of Deaths or afflict-

ing that point.   Death comes unseen on silent wings
& is not made known to the person whose chart it is.
However, we may read ahead to learn when the contingency registers in the circle touching somebody else
since the Moon by progression will continue to carry
the lethal power of the 8th House ruler to the planets she aspects, registering deaths in the circle as
long as the owner of the document retains ownership.

On April 16th, 1953, the Moon opposed the Part of
Deaths and squared Mercury in the house of friends &
a man friend passed away. In 1954 Mars ruler of the
10th (the death-8th for the 3rd-of-relatives) was on
the 11th cusp (death-8th for the family-4th), square
to the 8th cusp itself; and the 10th by converse motion in 27 Pisces came opposition Saturn in the 3rd,
timing the death of an uncle. An aunt died early in
1956 as the Sun in 27 Aries in the 10th was quincunx
Saturn while Mars-ruler-10th was still square to the
8th cusp - and the Moon in 12 Virgo squared the 6th,
which rules brothers and sisters of the father-4th.

Through 1957 there were four deaths of friends as
the Moon passed over Saturn-the-Reaper co-ruler 8th,
while Mars was still on the 11th and square the 8th.
The Part of Deaths in 13 Aquarius sesquared Saturn &
exactly semisquared Jupiter at the time, and we note
that Jupiter rules the 6th (the friends' 8th). They
were all middle-aged persons, as Saturn would show.

In 1959 six friends died as the Moon opposed Mars
and exactly paralleled him while progressed Mars was
exactly conjunct Mercury in the friends-11th. Venus
ruler 11th in 7 Gemini trined (D) in the 8th so that
death for these six women was peaceful in each case.

Remember, there must always be supporting aspects
to confirm each reading, such as we have found here.

Widowhood

When we speak of widowhood we draw attention to a triple indication of it in this chart. The ruler of this woman, the Moon, is in the HOUSE of widows (the 12th) square Neptune the PLANET of widows and square the Part of Fortune who is in close conjunction to a malefic fixed star, Vindemiatrix in 8 Libra - called the Star of Widowhood. The moment you see the ruler of the 1st in the 12th you have your first clue, and if there is emphasis on the 12th House or 12th Sign, Pisces, or its natural ruler Neptune, and especially if Vindemiatrix is also involved, you may assuredly forecast widowhood during ownership of the document. The Moon empowered by Uranus-ruler-8th reveals WHEN.

For the husband's passing on January 23, 1960, we note the Moon 7 Scorpio square the Part of Deaths in the 8th, the Fixed Signs signifying that there would be no avoiding it now. That it would be the husband is confirmed by the Converse Moon 27 Pisces, exactly opposition Saturn the planet ruling the husband-7th.

Grandchildren

With the maternal Sign Cancer rising and holding her ruler Moon trine Jupiter in the grandchild-9th, there would be grandchildren; although the square to Neptune co-ruler of the 9th reveals the death of one (Neptune in the death-8th for the grandchild-9th) by miscarriage, a Neptunian affliction, which occurred a few months after filing the document when the progressed Moon exactly squared Neptune. When the Converse Midheaven 28 Pisces conjoined Jupiter in the 9th, accompanied by the transiting Sun, her grandson arrived. Her granddaughter arrived 12 years before when the Converse 9th in 18 Aquarius trined Neptune.

On October 10, 1957 a great-granddaughter arrived as the progressed Sun in 28 Aries conjoined the mid-point between Jupiter & Venus and semisextiled both. By progression the Moon & 4th cusp conjoined Fortuna while the progressed Fortuna and transiting Jupiter were both together in 13 Libra for this Libra child.

On May 5, 1959 a Taurus great-grandson arrived as the progressed 9th cusp in 8 Pisces sextiled Mercury in Taurus, & the transiting Moon 23 Aries conjoined the Sun. The progressed Moon 28 Libra was quincunx both Jupiter and Venus. The quincunx is a "problem aspect" involving illness and at only 2 weeks of age he underwent an internal operation for pyloric stenosis. The transiting Jupiter 28 Scorpio trining Jupiter in the 9th blessed him with a speedy recovery.

The compensation Jupiter gives

This woman stands to gain continuously during the life of the document because her ruler Moon is in a good-luck trine to Jupiter-of-increase who is exactly sextiled by Venus in Taurus of money & valuables. She often came to the financial aid of those in need only to receive large sums, jewelry, valuable equipment and furnishings through unexpected and entirely unrelated sources. At the time of the flood-control work mentioned earlier, the property disruption signified by the progressed 4th in 5 Libra square Uranus in 1956 was recompensed in 1957 as the progressed 4th in 6 Libra conjoined Fortuna, bringing compensation in four figures, more than was paid the others, and entirely without effort or pressure on her part. Thus do we see the value in reading document charts.

* * * * *

BIRTH OF WIFE IN HUSBAND'S CHART

Natal chart June 21, 1901

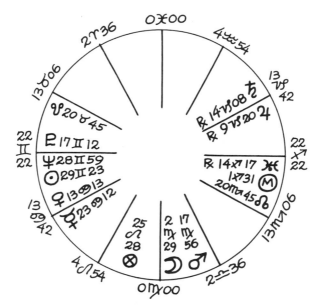

The fate of any marriage is also revealed. Here, the Part of Marriage (1st plus the 7th, minus Venus) 1:31 Sagittarius moved to square the Moon in the 4th denoting domestic discord. Venus opposition Saturn chills love, but the Moon trine Saturn from the 4th continued the cold domesticity for 24 years from the marriage Nov. 24, 1921 to the divorce Oct. 25, 1945.

THE BIRTH OF THE WIFE IN THE HUSBAND'S CHART

It would appear that Junius B. Smith, astrologer and writer, was first to advance a method by which to determine the birthdate of the wife in the husband's natal chart, work in this research also being done by George J. McCormack, Astro-meteorologist who provides a professional long-range weather forecasting service across the country, and who wrote on the subject around 1941. In the main, they took note of the position of the 7th-House ruler and its distance from the Midheaven, adding or subtracting the arc in months & days to or from the native's date of birth.

In this writer's research however a more extended method is employed, and while it may not be cricket for a woman to deliberately put into a man's hands the means by which he can ferret out the real age of the terminological inexactitudinarian he married – yet (by looking at it from a purely scientific viewpoint) here is the way to catch up with the fibber.

The year in his chart when there is a major progressed aspect to Venus, to the 7th cusp, to the ruler of the 7th and/or to a planet in the 7th, is the year of the wife's birth. If formed by converse motion, she is that much older than he.

In the chart opposite, the significators are Venus, the 7th cusp and Jupiter in and ruling the 7th. His natal ephemeris reveals that one day after birth (that is, one YEAR after or 1902) the 7th cusp in 23 Sagittarius aspected his own ruler Mercury; and also Venus in 14 Cancer and the Moon in 14 Virgo aspected both Saturn and Uranus, rulers of the ceremonial-9th promising a marriage ceremony with one born in 1902. As promised, his wife was born in 1902, on May 21st.

BIRTH OF WIFE IN HUSBAND'S CHART
Dwight D. Eisenhower
Natal chart Oct. 14, 1890

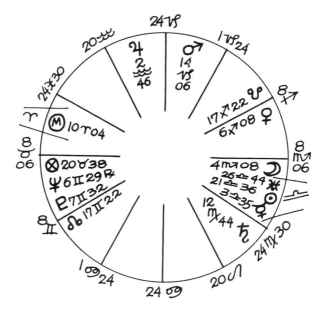

The significators are Venus, Mars & the 7th cusp.
6 days after his birth (6 YEARS or 1896) Venus 10:11
Sagittarius aspected the Part of Marriage 10 Aries &
Fortuna in 6 Gemini aspected Venus in the 7th, while
the ritual-9th in 7 Capricorn aspected Pluto coruler
of the 7th, and Mars ruler 7th aspected the nodes.
His wife was born as promised in 1896, on Nov. 14th.

A MAN'S NATAL CHART

March 16, 1870

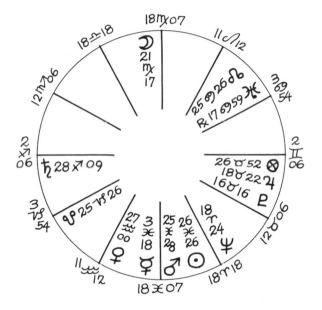

The significators are Venus, the 7th and Mercury, its ruler. 16 days after his birth (16 YEARS, 1886) Venus 2 Pisces aspected the 7th & its ruler Mercury, who in 0 Aries was parallel the Sun ruler 9th, while the Moon 3 Taurus aspected Mercury ruler 7th.   The wife was born on October 13th, 1886, 16 years later. The marriage lasted 32 years from January 2, 1921 to his death April 16, 1953. The Moon first over Saturn delays marriage so that he was age 51 at the ritual.

THE DUKE OF WINDSOR

June 23, 1894

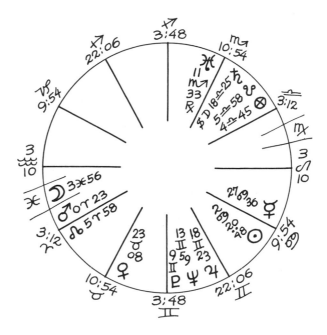

The significators are Venus, the 7th & its rulers the Sun and Mercury. His natal ephemeris shows that 2 days after birth (2 YEARS or 1896) Venus 26 Taurus was almost exactly sextile Mercury co-ruler 7th who, entering Leo, trined Mars who rules his ritual-9th. The Sun ruler 7th in 4 Cancer trined the Moon, while the 7th itself in 4:45 Leo was exactly sextile Fortuna in the marital Sign Libra. As was promised, the Duchess was born in 1896, two years after the Duke.

KING GEORGE V of ENGLAND
Father of the Duke of Windsor
June 3, 1865

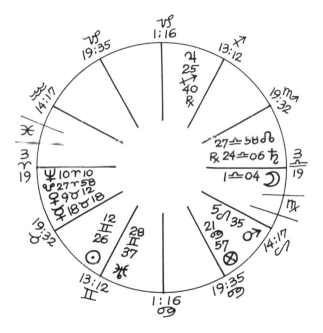

The significators are Venus, Saturn and the North Node in the 7th, and the 7th cusp itself. His natal ephemeris shows that 2 days after his birth (2 YEARS or 1867) the Moon conjoined the good node in the 7th and sextiled the Part of Marriage 27 Leo, while the Sun paralleled Jupiter in the ritual-9th, & the cusp of the 7th in 5 Libra sextiled Mars-ruler-Ascendant. His future queen, Mary, was born on May 26th, 1867.

3:40:44 pm LMT
Jan. 15, 1920
87W19 .. 38N46
(4025 C/Log)

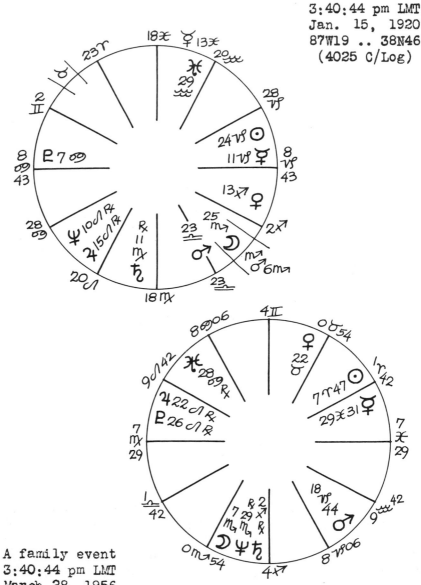

A family event
3:40:44 pm LMT
March 28, 1956
87W19 .. 38N46

THE DIURNAL CHART

The Diurnal Chart is a one-day TRANSIT chart set for a person as though he were born that day, therefore we combine his original birthtime, latitude and longitude, with the date from the CURRENT ephemeris. Calculate only the Moon and any fast planet changing Signs, using the original Constant Logarithm; and if you originally used the birthdate and its following (or preceding) date, now use the transit date & its following (or preceding) date and the same figuring.

During those years in which the regular progressions indicate activity confirmed by the progressed Moon in her month-by-month motion, we want to narrow down the possible date of an event to a probable one based on a diurnal transit. That date will usually coincide approximately with a New or Full Moon that aspects the Ascendant or its ruler in the natal map, but it must also conjoin a natal or progressed planet in order to date the event exactly. Thus we see that the Moon of the lunation may be approximate but it must move forward to be exact on the event date.

For our first step, we note that the regular progressions in the natal chart on the opposite page brought Mercury to 13 Pisces square Venus - a strong aspect denoting the action we are to bank on for the event; it is our starting-point, based on 13 Pisces.

This is a very important development because Mercury rules an angle; it is unfortunate because he is in his fall by Sign and, being Mercury, will involve a document. It shows unhappiness and a loss because his square to Venus is contrary to the happiness and

gain that she would otherwise give.   Mercury is in
bad aspect to the 4th cusp but not to the 1st so the
native himself is not directly affected but a member
of his family will be. The 4th House will therefore
be the prominent house to read in the Diurnal Chart.

Seeking the progressed Moon for confirmation, we
take January for this man because she was 13 Pisces,
siding with progressed Mercury against Venus.   (She
had been in 13 Pisces before but not conjunct a progressed or natal planet; that makes the difference.)
We could have taken her in 13 degrees of any Sign.

Taking the ephemeris for the progressed year 1956
& starting with the birthday in January, we go forward through as many months as necessary to find a
lunation that squares or opposes the Ascendant.   We
want an afflictive aspect to agree with the square &
opposition Mercury made to Venus and the family-4th.

January had no lunation afflicting the Ascendant.
The February New Moon did not aspect the Ascendant;
the Full Moon did (5 Virgo) but by sextile, which is
not afflictive. The New Moon in March did not aspect
the Ascendant but the Full Moon in 6 Libra did, & by
afflictive square so that he was personally affected
and unhappily so to confirm the nature of the development in his circle that year, but indirectly since
Mercury's progressed force was directed elsewhere.

The Full Moon was on March 26th in 6 Libra but no
natal or progressed planet was there aspecting the
Ascendant; this was the lunation to tie to therefore
but not the date for it to register. We had to wait
for this Moon to move on until she met a planet that
did aspect the Ascendant - and this she did two days
later on March 28th when she came to the conjunction
of progressed Mars in 6 Scorpio trine the Ascendant.

We accordingly set the Diurnal Chart for the time
and place of birth (3:40:44 p.m. LMT at 87W19 38N46)
but the transit date March 28, 1956. Because we had
originally calculated the Moon for the birthdate and
the day after, we calculated her place this time for
the transit date & the day after, with the same Log.

Since the progressed planet was Mercury, ruler of
the natal 4th, we take the 4th in the Diurnal Chart,
and note its ruler Jupiter for the basis of what is
to occur, particularly as concerns the family. (Why
the family, instead of real estate or something else
also governed by the 4th? It is because Sagittarius
is there, a Common Sign, and they are the ones most
likely to signify relatives - therefore the family.)

Family affairs are shown to be extremely unfortunate here with the ruler Jupiter in the unfortunate
12th House of grief, square Neptune-of-funerals, and
exactly sesquare the Sun in the death-8th House; and
both Jupiter & the Sun in bad aspect to Venus in the
9th House of rituals. Fixed Signs denote that which
is inevitable and unavoidable, and the T-square here
falls out in Aquarius, the Sign of a cross to bear.
This is therefore a time of mourning, hence it is a
Diurnal death chart for someone in the man's family.

We conclude that it is the mother who is to pass
on, because the planet nearest the 8th cusp is Mercury, ruler of this mother-10th House; and the other
natural significators of the mother (Moon and Venus)
are afflicted by quincunx and semisquare to the Sun.

To make it easier to read the mother's affairs we
turn the Diurnal Chart so that the 10th cusp is rising as her Ascendant. The two malefics Saturn and
Neptune in her 6th-of-illness in opposition to her
Ascendant disclose serious illness because these are

major planets & otherwise afflicted (Neptune square Pluto, and Saturn semisquare Mars). The functioning Moon exactly quincunx the constitutional Sun denies normal physical co-ordination. Her ruler Mercury is very weak when detrimented in Pisces & about to pass out of the Sign: she herself is now "void of course" so to speak, so that her activity is about to cease.

We decide that it was illness and not an accident that caused her death on March 28th because Mars who rules her illness-6th is in her death-8th and Saturn who rules her death-8th is in her illness-6th. They are in mutual reception but by house only signifying an exchange of illness for death. If they were in mutual reception by Sign (which gets a person out of what he gets into) we would have expected recovery.

The observant student will want to know why we do not consider this the death of the native himself in the Diurnal Chart, since Mercury rules the Ascendant and is conjunct the death-8th cusp. It is because this is not a natal chart but simply a disclosure of outside conditions (transits) and is related to what his progressed planet rules in the natal chart: that planet is Mercury, not ruling his Ascendant & therefore not representing him: it represents his family.

Several confirming aspects for every conclusion we reach are a necessary and safeguarding requisite if we are to speak with authority. In this example, we might not have been so sure it was the mother and not another 10th-House person if it had not been for the inclusion of the other two mother-significators, the Moon and Venus, as well as Mercury-ruler-10th in combined affliction with the Sun in the death-8th.

☼ ☼ ☼ ☼ ☼

THE BEST SUBSTITUTE FOR A NATAL CHART

Probably the best substitute we can have for the natal chart when the time of birth is unknown is the Johndro Birth LOCALITY Chart, so called because it is set up for only the locality of birth & the date, dispensing with the time of birth and Sidereal Time, and with no calculation required for the planets. We take them unworked as at noon on the day of birth.

Our only calculation is in finding the Midheaven. This is done very easily with Right Ascension, which is the 360-degree distance from 0 Aries back to that same point. Any part of this circle is called ARC - and at the top of the Dalton Table of Houses we find it given with its equivalent in Sidereal Time: their mutual equivalent in Sign-&-degree is the Midheaven.

To find the Sun's Right Ascension, which we need, simply find a Midheaven in the same Sign & degree he is in and take its Arc for the RA/Sun, being sure to add any minutes he has, as:

```
March 11th, 1911 SUN Pisces 20 = 350:48 Arc
                             08 /     :08
                                  350:56 RA/Sun
```

Johndro completed this work in 1930 and used that year as the Base Year for this figuring & March 21st as the date beginning the year, with 29:10 Right Ascension of the Midheaven at Greenwich as it was then (being in 2 Taurus, which we do not require). Only three steps are required to change the year, date & locality to suit the person whose chart it is to be. Always begin by setting down the basic Line 1, as:

29:10 RA/MC Greenwich March 21, 1930

Right Ascension advances the Midheaven at the rate
of only 46.10 seconds per year. To change 22 years'
difference before or after 1930 to minutes, multiply
46.10" by 22 = 1014.20" & divide by 60" = 17 minutes
as shown by this Correction Table, saving your time:

46.10" CORRECTION TABLE

Yrs	Dif	Yrs	Dif	Yrs	Dif	Yrs	Dif	Yrs	Dif
1	00'	19	15'	37	28'	55	42'	73	56'
2	02'	20	15'	38	29'	56	43'	74	57'
3	02'	21	16'	39	30'	57	44'	75	58'
4	03'	22	17'	40	31'	58	45'	76	58'
5	04'	23	18'	41	32'	59	45'	77	59'
6	05'	24	18'	42	32'	60	46'	78	60'
7	05'	25	19'	43	33'	61	47'	79	61'
8	06'	26	20'	44	34'	62	48'	80	62'
9	07'	27	21'	45	35'	63	48'	81	62'
10	08'	28	22'	46	35'	64	49'	82	63'
11	08'	29	22'	47	36'	65	50'	83	64'
12	09'	30	23'	48	37'	66	51'	84	65'
13	10'	31	24'	49	38'	67	52'	85	65'
14	11'	32	25'	50	38'	68	52'	86	66'
15	12'	33	25'	51	39'	69	53'	87	67'
16	12'	34	26'	52	40'	70	54'	88	68'
17	13'	35	27'	53	41'	71	55'	89	68'
18	14'	36	28'	54	42'	72	55'	90	69'

Step 1 - Set down 29:10 RA/MC Grn March 21, 1930 and
add the Difference if after 1930 otherwise subtract.
            Now you have changed the year.
Step 2 - Always add the RA/Sun on the date of birth.
            Now you have changed the date.
Step 3 - Add the birthplace longitude if East. Sub-
tract if West.   This gives the RA/MC for the chart.
            Now you have changed the place.
The difference between this RA/MC and the RA in the
Table of Houses that is NEAR-&-LESS gives minutes to
add to the Midheaven.   Use the birthplace latitude.

April 16, 1854
89:39-W   40-N
A Pioneer Woman

Sun Aries 26 = 24:06
          09 ✓ :09
RA/Sun 24:15

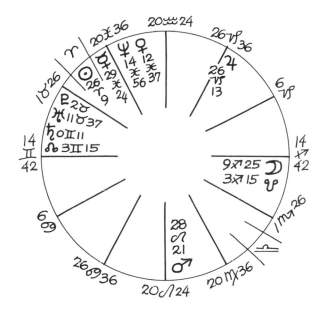

		3	2	1
Line 1		29:10	RAMC Grn Mch 21, 1930	
	−	:58	(Minus Dif. before ")	
		28:12	RAMC Grn Mch 21, 1854	
1930 Base Year	✓	24:15	RA/Sun April 16, 1854	
1854 Birth "		52:27	RAMC Grn Apr. 16, " 54	
76 yrs = 58'	✓	360:00	(in order to subtract	
		412:27	longitude this time)	
	−	89W39	Birth Longit (✓E, −W)	
For South Latitude		322:48	RAMC Birth Loc. Chart	
add 180:00 & start	−	322:24	Near-&-Less, 20 Aquar	
with the 4th cusp.		:24	Min. for MC 24	

The chart on page 133

The extraordinary accuracy given by the cusps and their rulers in describing the owner of a Birth Locality Chart, his life and interests, will be clearly shown in this example. As ever, our basic requisite in any chart must be the Signs on the angular houses and the facts revealed by their rulers & the aspects that tally with them and the Midheaven and Ascendant as events occur in the life.   These are major clues on which we rely for both delineation & forecasting.

Because Gemini is the rising Sign here it is safe to say that this woman is guided by logic that is on sure ground because the middle decanate denotes COMMON SENSE. She will succeed in life by using common sense in all emergencies because the 1st cusp trines the 10th-of-success, and her ruler Mercury is in the 11th-of-circumstances sextile the practical Saturn.

She will need common sense: she will often be at the end of her rope, so to speak, because her ruling planet Mercury is at the end of the Sign he is in, & will know sorrow and heartbreak because her ruler is in the sorrowful Sign Pisces, detrimented and marked for sorrow even before birth because last over Neptune, planet of misfortune who squares the Ascendant. The ups-and-downs of life that we call Circumstances will begin to register before her first birthday because her ruler Mercury is in the Circumstances-11th and will change Signs during her first year. When a natal planet is in (or enters) 0-degrees, there will be a major change in the life while only months old.

This is the chart of a pioneer woman who crossed the plains in a wagon train with her parents before her first birthday. The remarkable thing about this Johndro chart is the confirmation it gives. Mercury not only changed Signs but exactly sextiled Saturn - ruler 9th-of-travel & in the Sign of travel - while the Moon ruler travel-3rd opposed the Ascendant from the 7th-of-removals, showing changes in the environment because of removal to a distant place signified by the Moon being in Sagittarius-of-a-distant-place. Jupiter in or conjunct the 9th also shows a journey, breaking up the home by square to the Sun ruling the home-4th, thus confirming the accuracy of the cusps.

She had a good education and was graduated from college which was "a rarity for a woman of that era" but promised by Mercury's trine to the Moon ruler of the elementary-schooling-3rd in academic-Sagittarius and his sextile to both Saturn-ruler-academic-9th & the scholar-Jupiter conjunct the 9th. Note also the Sun in the intellectual Sagittarian decanate of the head-Sign Aries, trine Mars-ruler-6th by age plus-2: she was bound to apply herself very early in life.

On April 9th, 1873, she married; and in 1882 they settled on a ranch in open country in Nevada, a very dangerous locality where there were hostile Indians, as shown by Mars-of-danger in the home-4th where she would settle. Her home would stand isolated because the ruler of the home 4th cusp stands alone by Sign.

For marriage: the Moon came to 15:48 Leo & trined the marriage-7th cusp, matrimonial-Venus came to the conjunction of Mercury-ruler-Ascendant, and the 9th-of-rituals trined the Ascendant, confirming the correctness of the Johndro cusps. But tragedy was also shown by the Midheaven now in 9:24 Pisces, the widow Sign, square the Moon behind the marriage-7th. This is considered because the ruler of the Ascendant and the natural significator of marriage - Mercury & Venus - are both in the widow Sign with Neptune who is the planet of widowhood (showing how the marriage is

to end by being in the 10th which is the end-of-the-
matter-4th after the marriage-7th).   The "Finger of
God" double-quincunx aspect usually signifies widowhood when the rulers of the 1st and 7th are involved
especially with a malefic in the picture or Vindemiatrix, the Star of Widowhood in 8:41 Libra.   In this
chart, Mars is quincunx both Mercury & Jupiter, ruling the 1st & 7th, and square Saturn ruler death-8th
bringing violent death to her husband: on July 13th,
1883 he was murdered by a desperado.   Venus had progressed to 8 Aries opposition the Star of Widowhood.

Several weeks after her husband's death her fifth
child was born; he died at age 14 when Mercury ruler
5th-of-children was 9 Gemini, opposition the Moon; &
the Moon in 6 Cancer was opposition the death-8th.

As a widow, she brought up her children alone and
in that same isolated locality, developing the ranch
on a vast agricultural scale and hiring both Indians
and white workers.   She managed the enterprise without previous training or experience and provided the
produce required by the miners of the huge El Dorado
Canyon Mines.   Her ruler Mercury sextile Jupiter and
Saturn gave her good judgment and business acumen, &
Mars angular, trine and mutual reception the exalted
Sun gave success and the courage of her convictions.

She was a member of many clubs and civic organiz-
ations.   She died on March 6, 1926, her funeral pro-
cession being the largest ever witnessed there - Las
Vegas - and her entombment awaited the completion of
a vault hewn out of solid stone.   "Burial awaits" if
the ruler of the grave-4th is intercepted as here, &
if a malefic in the 4th squares Saturn, both showing
delay by holding in abeyance.   Saturn-ruler-8th now
opposed the Moon from 9:15 Gemini, and the Sun 5:26
Cancer exactly semisquared the end-of-life 4th cusp.

※ ※ ※ ※ ※

CORRECTING THE TIME OF BIRTH

When an important event in the life occurs, it is expected that the natal chart promised it & the progressed chart times it. This is a mathematical procedure, easiest seen by the number of degrees needed by the Midheaven or Ascendant to complete its aspect to a natal planet, thus timing the event. However, this number is usually only approximate - because in progressing the chart by the day-for-a-year method in the natal ephemeris we see that the sidereal time that moves the Midheaven forward is not that exact, and we always rectify a chart through its Midheaven.

First set down the original chart data, including the given birth hour and date, the latitude of birth and the longitude-and-EGMT, the Birth Sidereal Time and its date, the original Calculated Sidereal Time, and the Sign-&-degree it gave for the Midheaven, as:

5:57:55 a.m. CST 2/27/1898, 41N 91W03 (EGMT 6:04:12)
22:25:25 Birth Sidereal Time 2/26/1898
Orig. Calc. S.T. 16:23:07 and Orig. M.C. 7:34 Sagit.

Select an event shown by the progressed Midheaven aspecting a natal planet WITHOUT EXACTITUDE, and set down that planet's natal position by Sign-&-degree. Find the Progressed Sidereal Time for the age & note the Progressed Midheaven it gives & how many degrees it is off in aspecting that natal planet exactly: we call these the Adjustment Degrees. Add or subtract them to or from the incorrect progressed Midheaven to find the ADJUSTED Progressed Midheaven which does aspect the planet exactly. Add or subtract the same Adjustment Degrees to or from that incorrect Midheaven at birth to get the ADJUSTED Natal Midheaven.

The native left her birthplace at age 15 with the
progressed date March 14th in the natal ephemeris --
but we take the sidereal time for the previous date
because it was an a.m. birth and we originally took
the sidereal time for the day previous to birth. We
subtract the Birth Sidereal Time from the Progressed
Sidereal Time to find the increase in 15 years which
we add to the Original Calculated Sidereal Time to
find the Progressed Sidereal Time for age 15, giving
the Progressed Midheaven for the aspect. We want it
to sextile natal Mercury 24 Aquarius more exactly.

```
      23:24:33 Prog. S.T. Mar. 13th
   -  22:25:25 Birth S.T. Feb. 26th
      00:59:08 Increase in 15 days
   ⨍  16:23:07 Original Calc. S.T.
      17:22:15 Prog. S.T. at age 15
               (Prog M.C. 21 Sagit)

   Wrong Prog. MC 21 Sag (3-d short)
            ⨍   3 Adjustment deg.
   ADJ. Prog. MC 24 Sag sxt Mercury

   Wrong Natal MC  7:34 Sagittarius
            ⨍   3:00 Adjust/deg.
  *ADJ. Natal MC 10:34 Sagittarius
```

*When the Adjusted Natal M.C. includes minutes it
is between a greater & a lesser sidereal time in the
Table of Houses.   Find the Whole Difference between
these two and divide.   If the minutes are nearer 15
(1/4 of a degree) take 1/4 of the Whole Difference;
if nearer 30 (1/2 of a degree) take 1/2.   If nearer
45 (3/4 of a degree) take 3/4 of the Difference.   To
this, add the lesser sidereal time, from which subtract the Original Calculated Sidereal Time, to find
the correction-difference to add to or subtract from

the given birth hour to rectify it.   This gives the
rectified time of birth for the correct natal chart.

```
      16:37:42 S.T. for 11:00 Sagit
   -  16:33:26 S.T. for 10:00 Sagit
        /4:16 the Whole Difference
         2:08 half (34 min. on MC)
   /  16:33:26 S.T. for 10:00 Sagit
      16:35:34 S.T. for 10:30 Sagit
                  not 10:34
   -  16:23:07 Orig. Calc. S. Time
      00:12:27 difference to add to
   /   5:57:55 given time of birth
       6:10:22 a. m. CST, Feb. 27th

       6:10:22 a. m. CST, Feb. 27th
   -      4:12 for longitude 91W03
       6:06:10 a. m. LMT, Feb. 27th
   /  12:00:00 noon previous,  26th
      18:06:10 interval since  noon
          3:01 10-s corr. for int.
          1:00 "    for EGMT 6:04:12
   /  22:25:25 Birth S.T. Feb. 26th
      40:35:36 more  than  24 hours
   -  24:00:00
      16:35:36 Calc. S.T. MC 10 Sag
                             34
```

The Ascendant.

Sometimes it is the progressed Ascendant that is
making an aspect WITHOUT EXACTITUDE and should be in
an earlier or later degree than it is.   Remembering
that we always rectify through the progressed Midheaven, we look in the Table of Houses and under the
latitude of the birthplace locate the Ascendant as
it ought to be for that aspect.   That is the correct

progressed Ascendant, and the Midheaven accompanying it is therefore the correct Progressed-and-ADJUSTED Midheaven at the event: we note its Sign-and-degree.

The difference between the degrees of the Adjusted Progressed M.C. and the incorrect progressed M.C. is the adjustment-difference in degrees to add to or subtract from the incorrect natal M.C., thus finding the correct-and-adjusted natal M.C. as on page 138. Remember however that if you add at this point, you must add to the given birth time later to rectify it but if you subtract at this point you must subtract from the given time of birth later, to rectify it.

If there are no minutes in the Adjusted Natal MC, take the sidereal time accompanying it in the Table of Houses as the Adjusted Calculated Sidereal Time for the natal chart. The difference between it and your original incorrect Calculated Sidereal Time is the difference to add to or subtract from the given time of birth, thus rectifying it. If there are minutes in the Adjusted Natal MC it is between a lesser and greater sidereal time in the Table of Houses and handled as on page 139 herein, to rectify the time.

With her corrected birth hour 6:06:10 a.m. LMT, & Calculated Sidereal Time 16:35:36, set the cusps and work the planets for this woman's chart, and see how exactly it timed other progressed events. In 1933, at her father's death, the progressed father-4th was in 13 Cancer quincunx Mars (a death aspect), and the 8th in 28 Scorpio exactly opposed the Moon, ruler of his Future-2nd. In 1957, at her mother's death, the progressed mother-10th was in 5 Aquarius, square the Solstice Point of Mercury in the 8th (deaths in this native's circle) & the mother's 4th in 28 Taurus was conjunct the Moon-ruler-her-8th & sesquare the 8th.

✮ ✮ ✮ ✮ ✮

WHEN & HOW PROGRESSIONS OPERATE

The pinpointing of the actual culmination of an event denoted by a progressed aspect is not too easy even under apparently exact circumstances but we are more likely to succeed in our forecast if we keep in mind certain basic and requisite conditions.   These are dependable rules, very valuable to all students.

1 - First, no promise made, no promise kept: that is to say, if the two significators were not in any natal aspect however insignificant there was nothing between them at birth to bank on later and therefore nothing significant will happen between them later.

In this connection, insignificant aspects assume importance, and the student should acquaint himself with them all. Based on the semisextile of 30 degrees, add 6 for the 36-degree-semiquintile or 10 for the 40-degree-nonogon, or 15 for the 45-degree-semisquare. To the 60-degree sextile, add 12 for the 72-degree-quintile.   To the 90-degree square add 18 for the 108-degree-trecile. To the 120-degree trine, add 15 for the 135-degree sesquare.   The 150-degree quincunx is just one Sign away from the opposition on either side as: Sun 5 Aries, opposition 5 Libra and quincunx 5 Virgo & 5 Scorpio. 6 less than the 150-degree quincunx gives the 144-degree-biquintile.   These are in the MINOR CATEGORY but they do "promise".

Planets not in any major or minor aspect may yet operate if they are in parallel of declination, which is the equivalent of a benefic conjunction either at birth and extending throughout life or by progression and lasting for the whole period.

In the MAJOR CATEGORY are the conjunction, sextile, square, trine, opposition and the parallel.
See page 58 for the orb allowed all the aspects.

2 - The progressed aspect must be a major one for
a major event. Minor aspects by progression are useful to support or confirm the major progressions but
they otherwise require to be accompanied by a strong
transit to enable them to register in a major event.
Transiting planets come from the current ephemeris.

When an uneventful year seems probable because of
only minor progressed aspects, watch for the date in
the current ephemeris when a lunation or eclipse, or
transit of a major planet (especially one turning in
direction) falls on that minor progression, thus co-
operating with it and empowering it to major action.

The orb at PROGRESSION is usually given as 1 degree applying and 1 degree separating, amounting
to a 2-year period of waxing-&-waning intensity.
The planets vary in their motion, however, and a
check of the natal ephemeris will show the exact
number of days (called years) to allow for their
progressed area, of more or less than two years.

The Sun is always allowed 3 years: $1\frac{1}{2}$ before and
$1\frac{1}{2}$ after exactitude: still more for his parallel
to a heavy planet.   For instance, a child born
December 1, 1960 would have 31 years' Jupiterian
protection through adversity because the Sun and
Jupiter were in parallel of declination 31 days.

Whatever troubles come to a person through other
progressions, the natal Sun or Moon or ruler of
the Ascendant conjunct or parallel (or in mutual
reception with) the Greater Benefic Jupiter will
always see him through: even death will be easy.

3 - The natal aspect is likened to a bonfire laid
and waiting for something to set it off, and this is
done by a progression to it, which sets a prescribed
area or period of years (as explained on the preceding page, paragraphs 4 and 5) in which time the progression culminates in an event (or events: since it
can be stimulated into action as many times as it is
aspected by major transits during the period shown).

The more natal promises that culminate in events,
and the more transits that aspect the progressed in-
dicator, the more action there is during the period.
We note the nature of the natal aspect to see what
was promised, & the nature of the progressed aspect
to see how easy or how difficult it will be for the
person to handle whatever it is that is eventuating.

For example: the natal Sun applying to an aspect
of the planet ruling the 8th House, and now progressed to his 3-year area of action, telling us
that the natal promise is now ready to register.

If that natal aspect was bad it means an adverse
8th-House development such as surgery, taxation,
loss because of a death in the circle, etc.   If
the natal aspect was good, however, it now means
a desirable 8th-House development: financial and
material gains through other people, inheritance
or legacy, pensions granted, payment of debts or
refund of taxes, alimony, gifts and settlements.

The nature of the progressed aspect tells us the
way we will handle the adverse or desirable culmination of the original aspect. A square makes
us go to extremes in overcoming obstacles in our
way now, so that the cost is greater. A trine is
just the reverse, thus we find the going easier,
the returns more gainful. The sextile is like a

lesser trine.   The conjunction and the parallel bring co-operation from others and affiliations, but the opposition refuses these, and separative action develops.   A quincunx is a minor aspect & involves a period of reorganization in handling the natal promise (and supporting someone else).

4 - Several kinds of outside stimulation are possible, from which to derive the event-date we seek.

The YEAR in which any progression is within orb of aspect is the approximate year of the event, if activated by outside stimulus: otherwise, we await another year within that progressed area.

The MONTH of the event that year is usually when the progressing Moon reaches her month-by-month-degree that aspects the progressed significator, but not necessarily - a transit may be stronger.

The DAY may be set by the Moon or major transit. The month starts with your birthday-of-the-month & if the month-by-month Moon's degree that month is in major aspect to the progressed aspect, the event may happen that DAY, as timed by the Moon. If her aspect is minor, the DAY of that month is generally set by a major transit activating that Moon or either party to the progression itself.

Transiting Mars or a total or partial eclipse on or afflicting a natal malefic will register immediately if the Sun, Moon, ruler Ascendant or a planet angular is afflicted by progression that year and particularly that month.   At such times Mars has extraordinary, dynamic force capable of "getting into the fight" to precipitate disaster and the more so if it happens in angular houses. The angular houses all afflict the First House.

When two planets of contradictory natures join
as a stimulating transit (such as Saturn & Mars)
whatever transpires during the progressed period
follows their contradictory lead. There will be
forward development and then backtracking with a
baffling effect of lost motion, foolish actions,
delay and frustration. If the progressed planet
they conjunct is in good aspect to the planet it
aspected natally, however, patience will repay.

A transiting planet changing direction to either
retrograde or direct on a progressed planet will
stand stationary there awhile and thus emphasize
the effect of the transit. This is shorter with
Mercury & Venus but quite long with Uranus, etc.
and the nature of the planet will be noticed for
a longer time, being held for the extra period.
With Neptune, subterfuge and double-dealing will
be more apparent; with Uranus, some vexation and
upsetting of the apple-cart; with Pluto, a group
complication slows the procedure, & there may be
many absences at the wrong time, more noticeable
for a longer period because of being stationary.

Progressed Mutual Receptions

This writer has observed an unusual situation in
which two natal planets in no zodiacal aspect but in
each other's natural Sign so that they are also read
as though back in their own, may progress to form an
interesting development. For example, Mercury in 10
Aries and Mars in 25 Gemini may be also read as Mars
in 25 Aries and Mercury in 10 Gemini.   When Mercury
progresses to 25 Gemini conjunct natal Mars he forms
an aspect to Mars' mutual reception place, 25 Aries,
making him favorably inclined toward taking part in
a development always having to do with an exchange.

☆ ☆ ☆ ☆ ☆

A LIFE CYCLE CHART

5:24 a.m. CST March 11, 1951 87W39 41N52

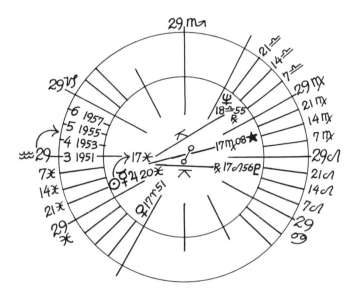

For the year of great peril in this native's life shown at age 3 by the Converse Sun opposing the Part of Peril in 17:08 Virgo - and setting off the double quincunx to Neptune and Pluto - note that at age 18 the progressed Ascendant 17 Pisces will do the same.

THE YEAR OF GREATEST PERIL

In her article appearing in the A. F. A. Bulletin
in 1955, Louise G. Mench LMAFA, delineated the chart
of a little girl who was so terribly injured in an
accident, suffering permanent and total disabilities
for which the city of Chicago was sued for a million
dollars in damages. Mrs. Mench invited the opinions
of others in answering the question as to whether
this disaster could have been foreseen, which is the
reason for presenting the Life Cycle Chart opposite.

A special chart such as this is of great value in
showing the event periods in the person's life, this
work being based on research by E. Baktay, Glahn and
others. The Ascendant in the natal chart gives the
Sign and degree for the Ascendant in the Life Cycle
Chart, using the same degree for the remaining cusps
with the Signs following in their natural order. It
will be seen that there will be no intercepted Signs
in such a chart and that it is possible for a planet
close to the cusp of one house in the natal chart to
appear in a different house in the Life Cycle Chart.
This affords additional insight into certain events.

Each quadrant measures 25 years of life, and each
house 8 years 4 months. Each of the four sections
in each house measures 2 years 1 month starting from
the Ascendant and the date of birth; but the accumu-
lation of 12 months gives an added year so that each
January moves forward 3 years 1 month instead. The
Ascendant moves BACKWARD in the Signs and in passing
through the sections it indicates the year in which
it sets off whatever aspects it contacts. Only the
salient part of this chart is given for this tragedy
but you should complete yours entirely, in order to
know where your progressed Ascendant is at any time.

The Cycle Chart should show the Part of Peril (P) taken from the natal chart (Ascendant plus the ruler of the 8th, minus Saturn) which is 17:08 Virgo here, since the natal Ascendant is 29:00 Aquarius, the 8th in Libra is ruled by Venus 17:51 Aries, while Saturn is in 29:43 Virgo. Any progressed affliction to (P) denotes a time of danger which is major or minor depending on the nature of other progressions at work.

On October 4, 1954, age 3½ years, little Patricia was run over by a city truck. She lost her left leg and then the thigh and part of the pelvis, suffering great internal injuries and facing a major operation on the female organs when she reaches age twelve.

In October 1954 her progressed Ascendant was in the 1953/54 section in 17 Aquarius opposition Pluto, ruler of her career-10th, meaning that at age 3½ she was to be deprived (oppositions are separative) of something of sufficient importance as to affect her life's ambitions or her self-supporting opportunity. At the same time, its sextile to Venus and trine to Neptune in money houses showed financial recompense.

In seeking confirmation in the chart, we look for whatever else has moved by the same arc 3½, and find that the Converse Sun 17 Pisces opposed the perilous point and compounded the menace by also forming the so-called Finger-of-God aspect, the double quincunx, to Pluto and Neptune. This showed a disastrous year of great danger, definitely indicated in advance and clearly foreseeable - but as to preventing the accident itself, that is something else again: it is the Finger-of-GOD aspect & apparently not in our hands.

It seems that all roads will lead to Rome at such a time, no matter what detour we make to circumvent Fate, so that nobody need reproach himself for what must be unavoidable or inevitable. Patricia herself would go out of her way to meet the danger that her chart showed was waiting for her: her scriptures had to be fulfilled. Thus, she inevitably strayed to an alley behind her home where the inevitable occurred.

On the other hand, foreknowledge is valuable because it gives us time for preparation, financial or mental, for what is coming, thus lessening an impact or affording the best care, or salvaging what we can under the circumstances.   Patricia at $3\frac{1}{2}$ could not know this, yet mitigation was provided for her by the concurrent good aspects in operation.   Her protection lay in having the Sun exactly conjunct the Greater Benefic Jupiter, especially in the physical First House, and at the time of the tragedy her progressed Ascendant (Life Cycle) exactly sextiled Venus the benefic ruler of the decanate rising at birth.

The alert student who observes that Mercury, who rules the death-8th, was also involved directly with the Sun because by converse motion he was also 17:00 Pisces opposition the Part of Peril, and may ask why death did not take place then, should remember that the 8th House does not always signify death of the entire body: it also rules any kind of surgery which involves the removal of a part of the body resulting in the 8th-House death of the part removed, as here.

Patricia is a bright and happy, even merry, child getting about on crutches.   The triple conjunction of Sun-Mercury-Jupiter at birth blesses her with the happiness, gayety, optimism & compensation for loss all through life that buoy her up now.   Always look for such saving grace in a chart afflicted at birth, and when the Life Cycle Chart indicates a dangerous, possibly fatal development, count heavily on what is protective, in your effort to comfort and encourage.

☆ ☆ ☆ ☆ ☆

The Arabian Points (Parts)

The Arabian Points (also called Parts) are arith-
metical degrees arrived at by using particular cusps
and planets for particular relationships. We always
use the number of the preceding Sign in the first 3
steps because the Sign that is named is not complete
but the number of the Sign in the last step has been
completed and the answer has gone into the next Sign
so we count off the number shown & use the Sign that
follows it. Aries will be represented as 0-degrees.

```
                         S  dg  mn
        Leo Ascendant    4  06:44
    ✠   Aries Moon       0  15:06
    =                    4  21:50
    -   Taurus Sun       1  19:08
Part of Fortune (3) 2:42 Cancer
```

The Ascendant plus the Descendant and then minus
the marital Venus gives the Part of Marriage (M).

The Ascendant plus the acute Mars and then minus
the chronic Saturn gives the Part of Sickness (S).

The Ascendant plus the death 8th and then minus
the functioning Moon gives the Part of Deaths (D).

The Ascendant plus the planet ruling the Sign on
the 8th cusp and then minus Saturn gives the Part of
Peril (P). If conjunct the Ascendant and also badly
aspected to a malefic it denotes great peril & major
injury; otherwise it is usually minor in comparison.

The Ascendant plus the Moon-of-functioning, minus
Saturn-the-Reaper "reaps" the Part of Legacies (L).

✾ ✾ ✾ ✾ ✾ ✾

THE PLANET'S DEGREE IS YOUR AGE AT EVENTS

By extensive research and thorough investigation, it is too evident to be a matter of mere coincidence that the degrees held by the natal planets and major cusps represent the native's age at events occurring in his circle during his lifetime and involving him.

Since the degrees in a Sign go no farther than 30 we multiply the planet's degree by 2, then 3, and so on, to find additional events past age 30, considering 90 years as a reasonable life expectancy. 0-degrees denotes an event before the first birthday and while the native is still only months old, and it is not responsive to multiplication. The degrees may also be divided instead of multiplied, to find early events or to note any agreement with a natal degree, confirming an event or giving it greater importance.

It is always worthwhile to list your known life-events, together with the dates, for probable use in later research work along different lines. In this particular work, it is especially time-saving to us.

Example:

Woman born in 1893 with a planet in 8 degrees in the 3rd House (brethren, neighbors, short distances) which planet rules the husband-7th. Another planet also in 8 degrees gives double emphasis on multiples of 8 so that the events would be important: it would thus pay to progress the chart for the years stated.

At age 8 (1901) her younger brother was born (important because he was given into her sole custody 2 years later at her age 10 when the mother died). At 16 (1909) the family moved a short distance away. At

age 24 (1917) her elder brother was killed in action
in World War I.   At age 32 (1925) she moved into her
own home in the same city. At age 40 (1933) 28 fire-
fighters died fighting a canyon park fire adjoining
her home. At age 48 (1941) her husband suffered the
first of many heart attacks which took his life some
years later.   At age 56 (1949) her younger brother
underwent surgery. And at age 64 (1957) her husband
suffered a major stroke invaliding him from then on.

Note that these ages are multiples of 8 degrees.

The houses in which the Sun, Moon & ruler of the
Ascendant are found explain important events related
to what those houses rule.   This woman was born with
the Moon ruling the Ascendant and in the 8th.   This
is the house of gifts from others, surgery, death in
her circle; and being 4th after the 5th it discloses
how love-affairs and engagements will end.   The Moon
is in 6 degrees, so we will use 6 and its multiples.

At age 6 (1899) her father's mother died.   At age
12 (1905) a girl friend in her circle died.   At age
18 (1911) she broke her engagement to marry.   At age
24 (1917) we have additional testimony of the death
of her elder brother.   At age 30 (1923) she received
magnificent gifts including $1,000 cash.   In 1929 at
36, she had surgical extraction of two molars. There
seems to be no notice of what occurred in 1935 at 42
but belated news of missing relatives abroad may yet
come. (For unknown events, we still list the year &
age, pending possible later disclosure of an event.)
At age 48 (1941) she underwent dental surgery again,
for a wisdom tooth. At age 54 (1947) she received an
appreciation-gift of $1,000 from a relative.   At age
60 (1953) she made a pilgrimage to the grave of her
mother, last visited 24 years earlier. Based on the
preceding events, age 68 (1961) must also register.

The degree on the Ascendant is also the basis for
personal and physical events in the life.   For this
woman, 13 degrees rising denotes age 13 (1906) while
she was living in San Francisco and went through the
earthquake and fire there.   For age 26 (1919) there
is no listing.   At age 39½ (1933) she went through a
severe earthquake in Los Angeles. At age 52 (1945)
she was on crutches for three weeks after a bad fall
& this exact event happened again at age 65 (1958).

As a rule, the Midheaven is taken for a man since
it is a business & career house, and the 4th cusp is
taken for a woman and her more-domestic life (but if
she is a career woman take the matters of the 10th).

The 4th rules real estate, the home & family, and
the father.   This woman's 4th cusp is in 29 degrees
and at age 29 (1922) she moved the family across the
continent. At age 58 (1951) she moved to a new home.

The planet ruling her 4th cusp is in 18 degrees,
in the 9th House of new neighborhoods (for the home)
and grandchildren (for the family) and sickness (for
the father).   At age 18 (1911) she left home & moved
to another State.   At age 36 (1929) she moved again
and to a distant city.   At age 54 (1947) she built a
home in another city.   These were all home events.

For the father, the ruler of the 4th in his house
of illness in 18 degrees timed his extreme emotional
upset at her age 18 (1911).   At her age 54 (1947) he
became incurably ill, and underwent surgery in vain,
passing away three years later as denoted elsewhere.

We said that the house the Sun is in refers to an
important event.   In 23 degrees in the 9th-of-grand-
children, we note the birth of the first grandchild
at age 46 (1939), which is a multiple of 23 degrees.

✸ ✸ ✸ ✸ ✸

CHART FOR A WEDDING CEREMONY

11;50;00 a.m. EST December 17, 1913, 74W 41N

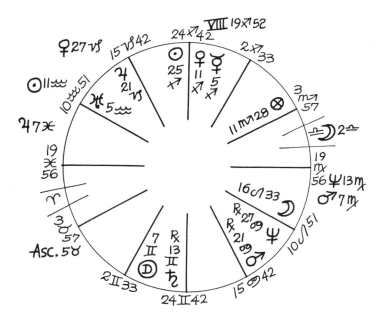

A continuous line of parallels

Moon 18, Uranus & Mercury 19, Neptune & Saturn 20,

Venus 21, Jupiter 22, the Sun 23, Mars 24.

THE WAY OF A MARRIAGE

The chart for a wedding is always set for the moment the groom & bride are pronounced husband & wife as in the chart on the opposite page. We note which planets rule the Ascendant & any intercepted Sign in the 1st House to represent the groom; here, they are Neptune & Mars. The Descendant and any intercepted Sign in the 7th House designate the bride's rulers: here, they are Mercury and Venus.

The 9th House rules weddings: that is, the formal ceremony legalizing a 7th-House union that is otherwise a "common-law" marriage. In this instance, two rulers of the 7th appear in the same Sign in the 9th and account for two ceremonies for the one marriage. This one is the Mercury-ruled formal ceremony and it was performed by a Chief Justice in his robes, as we may expect when Jupiter rules the formal 9th and is in the judicial Sign Capricorn. The second ceremony is the Venus-ruled Jewish orthodox ritual, performed under a chuppah (decorated canopy), a ritual of very great beauty and formality in which gayety, feasting & dancing around the couple had their Venusian part.

The 9th House also rules distant places & foreign shores, so that the ruler of the marriage-7th in the 9th is indicative of marriage of a couple from different countries, which is the case here, & the more certain because in Sagittarius, the Sign of "foreign import" of any kind. (In a woman's natal chart, the Sun in the 9th (or the Moon there in a man's natal chart) denotes marriage to one from a distant place or different country if confirmed by additional testimony such as Venus in Sagittarius, or the ruler of the 7th in the 9th or 3rd House or Sagittarius, or a planet in the 7th House & in Sagittarius.) We note that the Part of Marriage is in Sagittarius here.

The groom's financial condition is shown by the 2nd, & the bride's by the 8th as a dowry. His money is very limited here because Venus its ruler is in a separative aspect to limiting Saturn (who holds back more when he is retrograde and also in bad financial semisquare aspect to the groom's own ruler Neptune).

The Part of Fortune in the 8th brings a dowry but not very large because it is squared by the Moon-of-functioning. It amounted to only a few hundred dollars' savings and went into joint-ownership at once because Mars disposes of it and is conjunct Neptune ruling the groom and in the community-property 5th. It would be used for furnishings because in the domestic Sign Cancer, and probably second-hand because in a Pisces decanate (Sign of the feet) meaning that they were "on their last legs" so to speak, when the planet is retrograde, denoting a weakened condition.

For the financial indications for the future, the 11th is taken, being the end-of-the-matter-4th after the 8th, revealing how the matrimonial finances will eventuate. If the Sun, Jupiter, Venus or Fortuna be there, reasonable wealth is promised according to the couple's sphere in life, which is determined by their natal charts: we note the strength or weakness there of the planets ruling or in the 2nd House, and always any benefic in the 10th at birth, so that any poverty or wealth is comparative in a wedding chart.

In this chart, we find Jupiter in the 11th which is the income-2nd of the groom's employment-10th and it is parallel the Sun in the 10th and trine to the marriage-7th cusp: the husband's industry will bless the marriage financially, therefore. Some blessings are always bestowed in life by Jupiter and the Sun - even if we count nothing more than life itself - and always much more when these two are in good aspect.

Gain by career is confirmed by Venus ruler income
2nd parallel Jupiter ruler career-10th, promised for
the tenth year when she conjuncts the 10th House and
the Sun there, bringing a brilliant rise and a title
of 10th-House rank (professional) because the Sun is
in the high-ranking Leo decanate.   This was the beginning of his Certified Public Accounting success.

For the financial position at the end of the marriage the Sun, Venus, Jupiter or Fortuna in the 10th
(the end-of-the-matter-4th after the marriage-7th)
brings a settlement or alimony if the marriage ends
by legal separation or divorce, or inheritance if it
ends by death.   This is usually true of natal charts
also.   Neptune well aspected in the 10th may be read
like Venus - but if afflicted is read like the other
malefics when in the 10th, giving little or no support during marriage & limiting or denying financial
security of the survivor at death, usually requiring
that the wife must work outside the home thereafter.

Since most marriages have in the background the
wish to own a home, there is great promise when the
real-estate Sign Cancer is strong in the chart or if
the builder, Saturn, is in the real-estate 4th House
or in the Sign on that cusp, denoting that an estate
will be built up in time, as in this case.   We want
Cancer or a Cancer decanate on the 1st, 7th, 4th,
2nd or 8th cusp or holding their rulers; or the Moon
in Cancer or the 4th.   An Earth Sign on the cusp of
the 2nd or 8th or holding their rulers denotes possession of land.   This chart promises real estate,
and the couple owned much from the 13th year onward.

For children we take the 5th House and there will
be more of them if a Water Sign holds that cusp or
its ruler or planets in the 5th (especially Pisces),
but fewer in Earth Signs and still fewer in Fire and

Air Signs.   In this chart, a Water Sign on the cusp
and holding two planets therein shows more children
than might be expected with Virgo on the wife's cusp
so that there were three: one living (the Moon ruler
5th trine the Sun and always direct) and two miscarriages (two malefics in the 5th, both retrograde and
denied help by opposition to Jupiter). We note also
Mercury ruler of the second-child 7th in opposition
to Saturn a malefic who is semisquare Neptune in the
5th: and Jupiter ruler of the third-child 9th in opposition to Mars: these give confirmation. The Moon
or ruler of the 5th square anything in the 8th takes
away the hope of children. Neptune in the natal 5th
shows miscarriage or abortion, and a "wave" of these
if in the 5th in an ingress or general-public chart.

There is a continuous, unbroken line of parallels
formed by the declination of all the planets, from
the Moon 18, Uranus and Mercury 19, Neptune and Saturn 20, Venus 21, Jupiter 22, the Sun 23 to Mars 24.
This gave complete unity, faithfulness and fidelity,
accounting for their long life of 46 years together,
which is confirmed by their rulers Mercury & Neptune
almost exactly parallel, uniting like a conjunction.
Consideration, courtesy & generosity are attributes
of the Sun & Jupiter, who parallel his co-ruler Mars
and her co-ruler Venus, to ensure enduring happiness
with neither partner intent on ruling the roost..

Just as all marriages have their beginning, they
all have their ending, which we realize will be by
separate maintenance, divorce or death.   When there
is no threat to happiness we assume that only death
can part the two, so we enter the Part of Deaths (D)
in the wheel (see page 150). In this instance it is
7:20 Gemini on the husband's side of the chart: this
is only a clue, but semisquare his co-ruler Mars it
is injurious (a semisquare is injurious, not fatal).

However, the midpoint between his rulers Neptune and
Mars falls in 24:35 Cancer & the conjunction to that
point would mean danger. We realize that his health
will not continue to be as robust as hers, because
both his rulers Neptune and Mars are retrograde and
below the horizon in the weaker half of the wheel,
while hers, Mercury and Venus, are direct and in the
stronger half of the wheel. This also suggests that
she will "go on" in life after he "goes back" so to
speak, and will therefore outlive him. Nonetheless,
Mars also rules the death-8th and is retrograde, and
this means that Death holds back & comes much later.

The distance between the Part of Deaths and the
midpoint 24 Cancer is 47 degrees, which the Table of
Solar Arcs (at 0:59:08 per year) calls 46 years plus
a little over, past the 46th anniversary in December
1959 and entering 1960. He died on Jan. 23rd, 1960.
By Solar Arc 46:20 the Ascendant 5 Taurus was square
Uranus in Fixed Signs of that which is inevitable &
unavoidable and involves spasmodic action. The same
arc directed his new ruler Venus, his co-rulers Mars
and Neptune, the Sun, Jupiter & the 8th cusp itself
to the afflictions shown by their symbols around the
outer rim of the wheel. Note that the Moon was conjunct the midpoint between Saturn & Jupiter, & semisquare her own position in 16 Leo, the heart Sign: &
his death was due to a major spasmodic heart attack.

Marriage being a partnership, all these rules may
be applied to a chart for any kind of partnership
based on a contract or agreement requiring 9th-House
certifying or legalizing. In this way we can always
determine the progress of the partnership & evaluate
its desirable or undesirable features, besides being
able to accurately gauge its duration. A common-law
agreement or understanding merely dispenses with the
9th-House recognition but often is just as binding.

☆ ☆ ☆ ☆ ☆

A HORARY CHART

Where is the yardage material I bought?

11:29:00 a.m. PDST Aug. 10, 1955, 118W06 34N

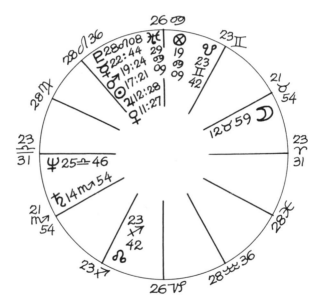

A horary chart is one set for the time of asking a question. The Moon is the significator & only her applying aspects from the Sign she is in are used.

WHAT ELSE DOES IT SAY?

When we have a horary chart to read we generally
confine ourselves to simply answering the question
alone as we shall do in the first part of this chapter: but many persons are so impressed that they are
eager to have additional personal disclosures, so to
their insistent "What else does it say?" let us follow up accordingly with the second part of the chapter. Incidentally, such additional investigation is
of inestimable value to the student of any branch of
astrology, sharpening his wits & enlarging his scope
of delineation, no matter what type of chart it is.

For Part One, then, the chart for the querent's
question is presented on the opposite page. Start
with the 1st, 2nd and 4th Houses and note the Moon's
aspects as listed in correct order below the chart.

The 1st House, Libra rising, rules the querent as
represented by VENUS in the 10th, denoting that part
of the home where she usually works. The 2nd House
with Scorpio on the cusp is the yardage asked about,
represented by MARS also in the 10th. The 4th House
with Capricorn on the cusp, SATURN ruling, shows the
possibility of mislaying anything proven not lost.
This is also the end-of-the-matter house and reveals
how the matter inquired about is going to turn out.

We have to establish whether the yardage is lost
or only mislaid, where it is and whether it will be
regained or replaced - and also approximately when.

MISLAID. The Moon last passed over Saturn-ruler-
mislaying-4th who is in the 1st House (with her) and
in the Sign on the 2nd (with her possessions) therefore she had it last & it is only mislaid, not lost.

The main significators are Mars ruling the yardage, Saturn who rules the mislaying, the Moon who is
co-significator in the matter and is also dispositor
of the Part of Fortune, and Uranus who receives the
Moon's final aspect. They are all in angular houses
and angular houses designate the home, therefore say
that the yardage is in the querent's home with her.

WHERE in the home? Mars ruler of the yardage-2nd
is in the 10th House denoting that part of the home
where the querent usually works with such things as
yardage. She uses the guestroom for sewing, and was
advised to search there in the northeast part since
the significator Mars is in the northeast Sign Leo.

WILL IT BE FOUND? Yes; the querent will find it,
because her ruler Venus moves to conjunct Mars ruler
of her possessions-2nd and will bring them together.
We find both Sun & Moon above the horizon, denoting
finding; one above and one below denote replacement;
both below, probably never found nor replaced.   The
Moon's final aspect is good (sextile Uranus signifying an unexpected turn) so it will be found suddenly
and unexpectedly. (The Moon last passed over Saturn
the mislaying & next passes over Uranus the finding,
which is another clue.)   Say yes, she will find it.

WHEN WILL IT BE FOUND? In a matter of hours, because the angles are in Cardinal Signs (the fastest)
and the Moon's first aspect is practically immediate
because it culminates in only two hours.   Note that
the Moon requires only two hours to move one degree.

At 1:30 p.m. PDST that same day the querent found
the yardage where she had previously looked in vain,
in a bureau-drawer and at the northeast wall of the
guestroom as forecast, among some wallpaper samples,
and passed by because it was rolled up as they were.

For Part Two, the chart has the usual interesting
points to bring out, many of which are as applicable
to the natal and progressed chart as to the horary.

You can say that here is a querent who is rather
pretty & has thick hair, because she is described by
the First House, ruled by Venus the planet of beauty
who in Leo has a lion's mane: and she is quite gray,
because Saturn grays when in the 1st House. She is
either too fat or too thin, with abnormal Neptune in
the 1st House (the body) and is in quite poor health
because the ruler of the illness-6th, Neptune, is in
the 1st square to the so-called incurable Uranus. We
also say that Saturn in the 1st denotes a disability
that is chronic in nature, but has been acute by the
past square from violent Mars. The Ascendant in the
same degree as the nodes is also bad for the health.

To answer: she is very much overweight: her ruler
Venus is conjunct the enlarging-Jupiter in big-build
Leo squared by the Moon who overeats in Taurus. She
has kidney and bladder disorders (malefics in Libra
and Scorpio in the 1st House and afflicted); and due
to a bad fall she has a spinal injury of long standing (Saturn-of-falls in the 1st squared by Mars in
the spinal Sign Leo) showing up as lameness & stiff-
ness which usually appear with Neptune and Saturn in
the 1st.   Saturn there denotes recent dentistry, to
be repeated as her ruler Venus completes her square.

She is becoming very forgetful, letting food burn
or boil over on the stove, and in many ways responds
to Neptune's forgetful influence when in the 1st and
particularly as the basis for this horary question.
She refuses to bind herself by making any promise or
plan, as denoted by Venus square Saturn-of-Time-and-
Plan, which unorthodox characteristic is understand-
able with Uranus highest. He signifies a free soul,

making personal liberty almost a career in the 10th, and certainly considering it of paramount or highest importance when he is higher than everything there.

She loves to travel, with the Gemini decanate ascending, the Ascendant trine the 9th cusp, and Venus her ruler conjunct the ruler of the 3rd House. She is frequently absent from home, because the restless planets Mercury, Uranus, the Moon and Mars are "out" when in the open, angular houses, as in this chart.

Venus in any bad aspect to Saturn shows a feeling of being rejected by someone of importance, which is true when she rules the 1st. At her mother's death, her father gave her for adoption at age three weeks, never seeking to see her again; and although she had sisters and other relatives none of them ever sought her out or demonstrated anything but rejection. We know that Saturn in the 1st quadrant denotes trouble in early life traceable to the father's misfortunes. Either Saturn or Uranus in the 4th or 10th signifies the loss of a parent by the time of the question.

When you see Neptune in the 1st, horary or natal, you know that there is something to explain about an early matter in the life, a name-change, the certificate of birth, and always a secret closely guarded. This woman keeps her adoption secret, and even today her husband & daughter do not know of it nor do they know her real given name or that she has had a birth certificate hidden among her papers all these years.

Saturn in the 1st quadrant shows hard labor early in life. She left school at 15 to work from 6:30 in the morning to 8:00 at night for $3.00 per week, six days a week, clerking, sweeping & even scrubbing, in a small country store. The person serves the public when the ruler of the 10th is in the "public" 7th.

In reading the 5th for children, she acknowledged that one was lost by miscarriage. Uranus rules this children-5th and is square abortive-Neptune. Saturn co-rules it and is square Mars. The Moon of conception squares Venus ruler of the querent & her power. Also, Neptune is abortive when afflicted in the 1st.

It is easy to see how high a place the remaining child, a daughter, has in the querent's life when we see Uranus, ruler of the 5th, highest in the chart. Nothing comes between them because the rulers of the 1st and 5th stand in wide orb of conjunction with no other planet between them. They live in different States as explained by the differing Signs but every six months they alternately cross the continent and visit each other. The yardage that the querent asks about is intended for a house-robe for the daughter.

For a number of years, the querent held a variety of jobs in order to finance the daughter's college education. If we turn the chart so that the 5th is rising as the daughter's Ascendant, the mother-Moon is in her schooling-3rd opposition Saturn in the 9th thus "going to great lengths" to provide schooling.

We find that the querent's future can be read in the horary, as well as her past and present. We say that within a month's time she will go on a journey, indicated by her ruler Venus moving to conjunct Jupiter-ruler-3rd in one degree, and since it occurs in a Fixed Sign and an angular house it measures to one month. It will be a longer distance because that is Jupiter's influence, but only for a visit because he rules the 3rd house of coming-&-going. Mercury also shows this by ruling the 9th & with only one degree to go to sextile the Ascendant, also only one month. (The querent left for the East Coast Sept. 19, 1955)

☆ ☆ ☆ ☆ ☆

CHART FOR A HYPNOTIC TRANCE

10:35 pm 11/29/1952   Pueblo, Colorado
3:12:42 Calc. S.T.   104W37 ... 38N17

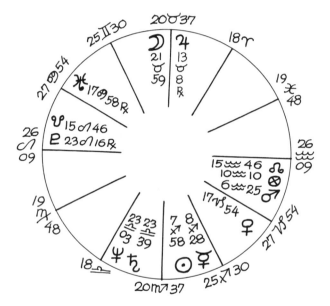

    The 7th House represents the hypnotized woman who says she was born Bridey Murphy 156 years ago and is now recounting events in her life at that time. She says she was the daughter of a lawyer and married to one at age 17. Note her ruler Uranus and Venus both 17 degrees, & her MC 17 from the Sun ruling her 7th.

IS IT TRUE, WHAT THEY SAY ABOUT BRIDEY?

When a book such as Morey Bernstein's "SEARCH FOR
BRIDEY MURPHY" precipitates so tremendous and wide-
spread a furore since it burst upon its astonished &
devouring public that it went into several editions,
and we are given precise data covering its important
astrological angle, the natural thing to do seems to
be to set a chart accordingly and see for ourselves.

By way of hypnotic trance, the subject Ruth Simmons was regressed or taken back into former incarn-
ations & specifically the one in which she was born
on Dec. 20, 1798 in Cork, Ireland, as Bridey Murphy.
She gave numerous names, dates & places, which have
been verified and a tape-recording of the session is
now available to the public. As astrologers, we are
mainly interested in determining whether the regression actually took place as discoverable in a chart.
Page 106 of the book gives full data for the trance,
as presented with its chart on the opposite page.

The 1st House represents the querent Mr. Bernstein
who asked all the questions: the 7th House is Bridey
who gave the answers. As usual, Mercury rules talk,
and since he is in distant-Sagittarius (mental journey) and retrograde (on the inner plane) & rules her
transition-8th (this 2nd) and is exactly semisquare
Saturn ruler of her 12th (the Past) he explains that
they are discussing her past-experience transitions.

For anything having to do with the unreal we look
to the shadow planet Neptune. Bridey's significator
Saturn is exactly conjunct Neptune, descriptive of a
person who is now one-and-the-same with unreality as
in a trance or dream state (being in her dream-9th)
and perhaps trying to see beyond the veil: certainly

in a hypnotic state as we read in a medical chart;
and as her ruler Saturn is in mutual reception with
obedient Venus in her friend-11th, she is obediently
following a lead.   The Moon's latitude is very wide
(5:00) giving one of them the opportunity to go very
far afield & to widen the scope beyond the ordinary,
which we know to be the intention at this session.

She said she died as the result of broken bones in
the hips following a fall.   Her ruler Saturn (falls)
exactly semisquare Mercury ruler of her major-injury
death-8th in the hip Sign Sagittarius bears it out.
She had no pain at death (her ruler exactly conjunct
comatose Neptune) & was fully aware that it was the
end (her co-ruler Uranus exactly opposite Venus who
rules her end-of-life-4th.   The opposition aspect is
like a Full Moon, giving light and awareness of what
is near).   Her husband was at church when she died
(Sun ruler her 7th in the church Sign), their rulers
in separate houses confirming that they were not together.   And she said that she came home many times
thereafter, shown by the mutual reception (exchange)
between Saturn her ruler and Venus, ruler home-4th.

The student may ask how it is that we read today's
planets for the past as well as for the present set-
up.   The answer is, that the planets in a regression
chart explain both time present and time past SO FAR
AS HYPNOTIC TRANCE STATES ARE CONCERNED, because the
person is here physically and there mentally, at the
same time.   What is in his mind is revealed, whether
it is factional or fictional.   In this chart, we see
the absolute tie-up between what may be only fiction
and what the planets are required to faithfully por-
tray, true or false.   Whether the statements made by
Mrs. Simmons under hypnosis were her own or simply a
reflection of another's words (the original Bridey's
or the hypnotist's) they are undeniably shown here.

☆ ☆ ☆ ☆ ☆

YOU OUGHT TO KNOW BETTER BY THEN

One way to get better acquainted with your natal
chart is to ascertain from it the part of life in
each of the four ages of man that will start you off
well enough, will develop better, and will prove to
be best so far as learning from experience at that
part of life is concerned.   These cover childhood,
youth, maturity and old age - which is better called
seniority: by then, if ever, we should know better.

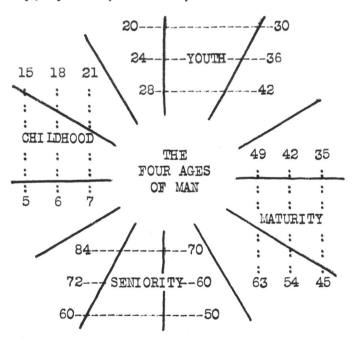

For this purpose, let us examine the diagram here
showing the quadrant for each period of life, the 3
houses each includes, and the approximate ages they
designate.   Read it as though placed over your natal
chart to find the ages where your planets denote future activity in the section they are in.   The more

planets in a section, the more you reflect your advantages at that period: and the more concentrated,
grouped or in sequence they are, the less you scat-
ter your forces.   The more planets on the Ascendant
side of the chart, the earlier you will be aware of
what you want in life & the longer your life may be.

Childhood

The years of childhood take in the 1st, 12th and
11th Houses from birth through ages 5 to 21, and involve the early environment (1st House) the mistakes
and disappointments (12th House) & the aspirations &
circumstances (11th) over which one has no control.

The middle years of childhood are centered in the
12th, where the adolescent feels under restraint and
most inclined toward disobedience & desire to be independent of adult authority & if there are planets
there he must learn to accommodate himself to rules
and regulations and not be his own worst enemy.   The
approximate ages 10, 12 and 14 are noteworthy.   The
closer he gets to age 21, the better able he is to
accept circumstances in general because he is in the
11th House of circumstances that he now understands.
He is still a novice, however, as he enters the next
phase of life, the 10th of integrity, success, whatever can raise him up (or cast him down in life when
he disregards such values and virtues).   No longer a
minor, he leaves the age of innocence fortified with
the power of any planet he has in the 11th House,
and by the lesson he learned there at age 18 or 19.
The succeedent 11th House ends the age of childhood.

Youth

The years of youth take in the 10th, 9th and 8th
Houses. From age 20 to age 42 according to where the

natal planets appear, the emphasis is on position in
life, the reputation, standing in the community, employment and development of talents that register in
worldly and business affairs (10th House) travel and
dealings with strangers: academic interests & ritual
participation (9th House) and responsibility for his
debts and obligations (8th House): remember that the
2nd rules what you own & the 8th rules what you owe.

The middle years of youth are centered in the 9th
where respect for the laws of God and man, known as
ethics, is his most important attribute since on it
hinges his right or wrong handling of the matters of
the adjoining houses, the 10th and 8th. Malefics in
this enthusiastic youth period promise a great deal
more than they deliver: if retrograde they withhold
a portion until they turn direct; & if well aspected
they give, but grudgingly; if afflicted, they give &
then take back. According to the house they are in
they threaten scandal, discredit, separation or divorce, dissolution of partnership, no gain by settlement or the law, and the death of someone important
in the native's private life & his immediate circle.
The approximate ages 25, 30 and 35 are outstanding.
The 8th, a succeedent house, ends the age of youth.

Maturity

The years of maturity take in the 7th, 6th & 5th
Houses, ages 35 to 63, indicating the action arenas
according to where either natal or progressed planets appear, more likely to be successful if benefics
or well-conditioned malefics are there and favorably
aspected. Dealings with others take precedence, particularly marriage, partnership & government service
(7th House) voluntary, co-operative work (6th House)
speculation, creative self-expression and parenthood
(5th House). The middle years of this part fall in

the 6th House, where service to others is the watch-
word, and specifically the persons of the adjoining
7th and 5th Houses.   The 6th is the house of whatever becomes habitual in time, so that planets here
denote a change in some theretofore-established condition, situation, custom or procedure. The approximate ages 40, 48 and 56 are noteworthy in this way.
The succeedent 5th House ends the age of maturity.

Seniority

The years of seniority (old age) take in the 4th,
3rd & 2nd Houses, ages 50 to 84, when future man may
achieve his best judgment based on experience, since
the middle years of this period fall in the house of
the mind and judgment, the 3rd.   Planets in the 3rd
give possession of the faculties to a good old age:
still longer as time goes on & the frontiers of age
keep advancing life-expectancy in general. This also
describes the native as a student all his life. The
3rd is the hinge on which the family-4th & substance
2nd depend: natal or progressed planets in the 3rd
protect the affairs ruled by these adjoining departments through the use of common sense.   Outstanding
ages in this respect are approximately 55, 66 & 77.
The succeedent 2nd House ends the age of seniority.

At age 91 the native enters the 1st House again &
embarks on his second childhood.   The stronger the
chart in its entirety, the longer the life will be;
and the more so with the Sun, Moon or ruler of the
Ascendant well fortified above the horizon at birth.

The turning points

The 11th, 8th, 5th & 2nd Houses are the succeedent houses of the chart - each one like a fulcrum or
base on which a period of life turns away from one's

childhood to youth, youth to maturity, and so forth, and the keyword is CIRCUMSTANCES. The 11th governs circumstances at a time of life when you take over the management leading to the 10th of credit or discredit, career, and matrimonial success or failure.

The 8th governs natural circumstances leading to the 7th of marriage, partnerships, contracts, agreements or compromises, lawsuits and the armed forces. Planets in the 8th will surely move into the 7th by converse direction, a motion not entirely favorable. If afflicted in the 8th they denote loss in the 7th.

The 5th governs non-dependable circumstances that are all purely speculative as to the manner in which they will turn out. Speculations, love-affairs and children, creative application - and all things that are bound to pass away when all is said and done because the end-of-the-matter-4th after the 5th is the death-8th. Speculative circumstances lead to founding a family or establishing a home (4th). Malefics in the 5th (or ruling the 5th and afflicted) are not completely favorable: disappointment usually ensues, real estate is not held for life, domesticity palls, one's pride in children is adversely affected, etc.

The 2nd governs self-preservation circumstances, based on material substance such as money, comforts, possessions & necessities of life, security, support and whatever talents can be turned to such account, leading to the personal protection the native needs.

Planets in the 11th, 8th, 5th and 2nd Houses disclose by their nature what you will do with them and by their character and aspects what they will do to your angular-house matters. If retrograde, you will not be fully prepared to enter the next phase, which is generally due to an adverse development in your life around age 21, 42, 63 or 84 when you were preparing to leave a circumstantial succeedent house. They are always the houses where we now know better.

All the ages we cite are approximate, indicating the general period in which planets in those houses will register. The ages designated in the diagram reveal that some natives retain their youth past 42, some reach maturity at 35, and some attain seniority early at 50. We pinpoint the actual age at events by the usual Secondary Method of progression, & also by directing (either direct or converse) on a Solar Arc (the Sun's daily motion of 00:59:08 as the planet's yearly motion). Major transits (conjunctions from the current ephemeris) bring outsiders into the circle, registering in your life at a definite time.

Ordinarily, you express yourself best & learn to know better according to where the ruler of your Ascendant appears & according to the planets you have in angular houses. Planets in mutual reception have a chance to express themselves in another period of life, also, according to where they appear when read as though back in their own Signs: show them outside the wheel and in color, for such reading. Benefics accord advancement and compensation for loss. Well conditioned malefics denote positions of trust & responsibility, although burdensome. Afflicted planets indicate periods of stress, tension, illness, sorrow or loss. But all the periods end in better understanding, so that we grow in judgment (and sometimes in spite of ourselves) - consequently, it is evident that sooner or later we ought to know a lot better.

* * * * *

YOUR PLANETS IN THE NATURAL WHEEL

The natural wheel has 0-Aries on the Ascendant & 0-degrees of the remaining Signs following in their regular order on the succeeding cusps. Set up such a wheel and enter your natal planets accordingly and we will see how clearly they explain much about you.

If your natal Sun now appears in an angular house (1st, 4th, 7th & 10th) it is also in a Cardinal Sign (Aries, Cancer, Libra, Capricorn). The keywords for such houses and Signs therefore apply to you, so you are alert, independent, preferring to do things your own way and having mental control over your physical reactions (1st); or representative of another person (7th) with some delegated control over his affairs; or one in higher office with some governing control in your own business or career (10th); or acting as subordinate head in national or family affairs (4th) where someone else has the deciding vote. These are the house-&-Sign combinations that denote publicity.

The Sun in a succeedent house (2nd, 5th, 8th and 11th) will be in a Fixed Sign (Taurus, Leo, Scorpio and Aquarius), giving you doggedness of purpose and building power which could be expressed in managing your own holdings (2nd) or those of a partnership or public type (8th); in speculative enterprises (5th), or in science or politics (11th). This combination has less publicity & more action in private affairs.

The Sun in a cadent house (3rd, 6th, 9th & 12th) will be in a Mutable or Common Sign (Gemini, Virgo, Sagittarius and Pisces), so you are quicker to adapt yourself to prevailing conditions and adopt improved measures & methods, clever & logical, mentally alert & willing to work harder than the others in whatever you undertake to do but usually working with others, which may be along clerical lines (3rd) or in widely divergent academic fields (9th), in serving or healing (6th) or in institutional work (12th) where your association is more likely to be with unfortunates. This combination falls between the private succeedent house and the public angular house, thus it is a mixture of both, denoting semi-public-&-semi-private matters and way of expressing them, almost always in a behind-the-scenes manner, like the cadent houses.

Where the angular houses and Cardinal Signs are the inaugurators or self-starters - & the succeedent houses and Fixed Signs are establishers of what has already been inaugurated elsewhere - cadent houses & Common Signs are the distributors, putting into circulation the methods & measures already established.

Now return to your natal chart & note which planets are Cardinal, Fixed or Common by Sign & angular, succeedent or cadent by house, & combine the effect by using the keywords in our preceding paragraphs.

For instance, a planet in a Cardinal Sign has the independence of the Cardinal Sign but its freedom of expression is determined by where it is. In angular houses, the independence is one-half originality and receives more publicity. In succeedent houses, the independence lies in furthering something the native did not originate: he shares ownership, so to speak. In cadent houses, the independence is within bounds as "the power behind the throne" obedient to others.

A planet in a Fixed Sign has determination rather than independence & is hard to dislodge. In angular houses it can be depended on to establish something already having a foothold, & his efforts are usually acknowledged. In succeedent houses, he consolidates

his hold on something already established, by building it up to his own advantage. In cadent houses,
he establishes something for general distribution or
general benevolent use, and works more in seclusion.

A planet in a Common Sign is the most adaptable &
impersonal of all, suiting his independence to whatever prevailing conditions or persons-in-command may
require: his independence is representative: it will
not endure. In angular houses he assumes borrowed
authority or pseudo independence for the time being,
which is only as good as it lasts. In a succeedent
house he is self-less in distributing something held
by others, independent in their name, usually having
to do with money or property. His independence in a
cadent house lies in taking charge when putting into
circulation the ideas, knowledge, writings, etc. of
others, and especially as reporter or ghost-writer.

Now evaluate the power of the planet itself as by
strength or weakness by Sign; direct or retrograde &
intercepted or free; in mutual reception; and by the
aspects it makes or receives. Its applying aspects
denote that the person is reaching out for something
more, while the aspects that it receives denote that
the person is to receive something more, & the house
the other planet is in reveals the source of supply.

If the aspect is good, the result is good; otherwise it is less favorable to some extent. Malefics
are harder to handle, & bring important developments
in the life. If strong by Sign they bring positions
of trust & responsibility: if afflicting the Ascendant they bring burdens. Benefics in bad aspect may
denote only that they give too much of a good thing.
The bad aspects usually "cost the person something".

☆ ☆ ☆ ☆ ☆

CHART FOR A TRAGIC EVENT

10:37:00 a.m. EST December 16, 1960, 73W57 41N

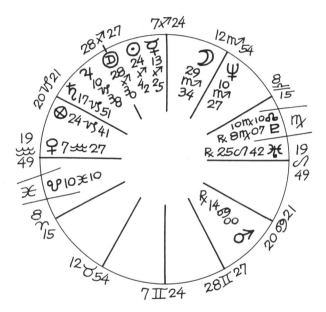

83 passengers and crewmen die as DC-jet airplane plunges to ground in Brooklyn street. Only one survivor, an 11-year-old boy who sustained a broken leg and critical burns, succumbing on the following day. Bad weather and snow hampered the flight of this and another plane: they collided in groping for landings at separate airports, each of them being off course.

TEARS FOR A LITTLE BOY

Who among us could read of the little boy who alone survived the terrible death plunge of an airplane that fell on a Brooklyn street, only to lose his battle for life the following day, without tears for him? Astrologers are a profoundly humane group, coming into direct contact with the scriptures that deal with their fellow-men, and if this were a natal or horary chart they would at once seek to find what solace they could, what consolation for the parents.

But an event chart is read differently. Here, the Moon is void of course (but is not so considered in a natal chart). In a horary chart it is read as "nothing to worry about because nothing is going to happen" -- but in an event chart it denotes that the activity now ceases and all is silence. The activity that has ceased is disclosed by the planet the Moon last passed over and the planet she last aspected. Here, they are Neptune and Uranus who are each in 13 degrees of declination, exactly parallel & operating as though conjunct for a disastrous turn of events. This writer has found that certain indications are always present either wholly or in significant number in any event chart to reveal what happened & how or why it happened. Let us therefore follow the clues present in the event chart on the opposite page.

Even if we were not told in advance that this is a fatal chart we would know it by the house where the rising Sign Aquarius belongs: the 11th where the Part of Death (page 150) exactly conjuncts the cusp, in the travel Sign. We turn to Alan Leo's "Degrees of the Zodiac," page 34 for 28 Sagittarius, and here is what it says: AN OPEN GRAVE AND A GREAT CONCOURSE OF PEOPLE, AND GREAT EXCITEMENT. A violent death.

We hope to mitigate this by the Part of Fortune
but in the 12th House or the 12th Sign Pisces or in
a Pisces decanate it becomes the Part of Misfortune.
Anything in the same degree as the nodes signifies a
casualty as Jupiter & Neptune here confirming death,
and anything in 29 degrees is at the end of his rope
as the Moon here, meaning finality in a death chart.

Whenever a mystery is involved, Neptune assumes
primary importance, being natural ruler of the 12th
House of that which is hidden from us.   If he were
in the end-of-the-matter-4th-House, something would
remain a mystery to the very end: this disaster will
therefore be solved. We get our exact clue from him
because he is singled out for our attention in three
major ways - as the planet last passed over by the
Moon, and as significator of the pilot by ruling the
intercepted Sign in the 1st House which is confirmed
by his Solstice Point (page 103) in 19:33 Aquarius
designating the Ascendant by being exactly conjunct.

Solstice Points signify something you don't see
at first, because they are not planets but hidden
forces. In bad aspect to Uranus here, the effect is
as though struck by lightning, stopping the pilot in
his tracks as it were. We know he is bewildered because his planet is Neptune parallel Uranus denoting
abnormal disturbance, so we look back to Neptune and
find that Alan Leo gives his degree in 10 Scorpio as
A MARINER'S COMPASS. Therefore the pilot's disturbance and that of his compass are one and the same,
and now we know what caused the disaster: a faulty
compass in bad weather, as shown by Neptune-of-fogs,
etc. "going dead" when afflicted in the 8th-of-death
and by semisquare to the otherwise-lightgiving Sun,
throwing the pilot's directive faculty out of focus.

To confirm it, Mercury is ruler of all delicate

instruments including the compass which does not operate so well when he is detrimented by Sign as here
and exactly parallel to Saturn since both are 22 degrees of declination: also, his Solstice Point is on
Saturn himself, so we see Mercury detrimented and at
the mercy of a malefic. We might almost say that the
compass is the scythe of the Reaper in this tragedy.

The saving grace for the child is shown by Mars
in the 5th-of-children in mutual reception (with the
Moon) which gets him out of what he got into.   But
the retrograde condition is always temporary & must
eventually change to direct motion, so that the saving grace accorded him is also temporary.   Confirmation of this is given by the child's ruler Mercury
exactly parallel Saturn who rules the child's death-
8th in this chart; also by the Sign on the 5th soon
to change: these "stay" the child only temporarily.

In a chart threatening danger, always show the
Part of Peril (the person's 1st plus the ruler of
his 8th, then minus Saturn).   It is (P) 28:27 Gemini
here, exactly conjunct the child's Ascendant and afflicted by the Part of Death opposite.   This always
describes one in peril and in great danger of death.
The little lad died the next day after the Moon went
over his ruler and as transiting Mercury & Mars were
quincunx (death aspect) to each other in the chart.

Why must we go to such lengths in our reading?
Because the astrologer must be diligent in seeking
every possible advantage for the child involved, yet
he must not be blind to such clear evidence as this.
It is a disservice to raise another's hopes without
absolute assurance - on the other hand, it is also a
disservice to be too quick in reading finality.   The
thing that gives us assurance in delineating a chart
is always the confirming configurations that we find

in several places, not just one, and this is true of
natal, horary, medical and mundane charts as well.

There will be other event charts in the future
that make us ask why, and for what specific reason,
and it will help the student to read them by following this simple formula: always note the planet that
the Moon last passed over and the one that she last
aspected, and whether or not she is void of course
completely or is saved by parallel to Fortuna. See
where the rising Sign belongs & note what that house
reveals. Look for any mutual reception in the chart
to give aid and to get the person out of what he got
into; and see if Alan Leo's excellent Degrees of the
Zodiac will afford a clue when applied to important
significators and cusps. For example, note what he
gives on page 9 for 7 Gemini on the cusp of the end-
of-the-matter-4th House -- SOME MYSTERY HERE WHICH I
DO NOT COMPREHEND -- which supports our selection of
the planet of mystery, Neptune, as the main significator in this tragedy. And finally, always insure
the accuracy of your judgment by clearly understood
confirmations that must be present in that chart.

The Ruler in Leo

I do not know if you have heard
  How dear you are to me:
It's in the singing of a bird,
  The rustling of a tree;
It's in the glory of the light
  That shines beyond the hill,
And in the whisp'ring of the night
  When all the world is still.

Bend to my heart your list'ning ear:
  That is a song of love you hear.

******

WHAT IS THE NATURE OF THIS EVENT?

An event is an actual occurrence that has definitely taken place at a certain exact time and in a certain exact location. An astrological chart set for that time and place will disclose the nature of the event itself and without any information or data being additionally accorded to the student excepting of course the special rules for this special branch. What happened is not told in advance to the student.

Being able to determine the nature of something that has happened can be vitally important in cases where circumstantial evidence damns an innocent person and the truth is urgently required.   It is also useful in clarifying other situations that have come to light, to explain conditions that prove baffling.

In order to be considered an event, it must be of general or extremely personal interest or importance and not an election or hypothetical question or some kind of assumption based on what appears to be true. Everyday actions or things done regularly are understood to be ordinary activity and cannot be singled out for special importance or considered as events - which are something unusual and out of the ordinary run of affairs; such as an accident, a record-breaking act or historical event, a catastrophe, disaster such as an earthquake or flood; a robbery, kidnap or anything warranted to attract our special attention.

To the student desirous of perfecting himself in the art of ordinary delineation of the various kinds of astrological charts, this is of great educational value because it heightens his powers of observation and increases his reasoning and deductive capacity.

The method to follow

An event chart is set up exactly as we do a natal chart, and the houses govern the same matters & persons. The usual meager list is greatly augmented in this branch however, and accompanied by full explanation where deemed necessary for beginners (as given on page 213, where rulership of intangible form is ascribed to the 11th House, being 4th from the 8th).

The time of the event must be accurately known in order to have an acceptable chart. If Saturn rules or is in the 7th House in any kind of chart there is sure to be an error in working the planets or cusps, or in entering the symbols in the right houses.   Go over the work again, very carefully, for exactitude.

The chart should be complete with the nodes & the Parts of Fortune, Marriage, and Death; and marked to show any conjunction or opposition to Caput Algol in 24 Taurus, the Pleiades in 29 Taurus or Serpentis in 19 Scorpio. These afford valuable clues in reading.

Enter the symbols for the Sun, Moon, Leo & Cancer in red in the chart, these being the basic points in this work.   Any planets in mutual reception (two in each other's natural Sign) are entered a second time in color outside the wheel in the same degree but in their own Signs. They denote changes & involvement.

Never give snap judgment.   Take time to examine all the points & have confirmation elsewhere before committing yourself. Use the keywords, & if in doubt use a general term rather than a specific one, until you have gained experience and confidence.   Do not deviate from the rules unless, of course, protracted and serious research on your part proves them to be faulty in some particular; infallibility is our aim.

The Four Significators

The EVENT will be of the nature of the house the Sun is in, and based on something ruled by the house where Leo is found. The ACTIVITY IN THE EVENT is of the nature of the house the Moon is in, and based on something ruled by the house where Cancer is found. Leo, the Moon & Cancer must confirm the Sun's event.

Each house is a department of many possibilities from which we are to eliminate all but the probable one. To do this we select from the matters ruled by the house the Sun is in the main possibility which is supported by the other significators as to house.

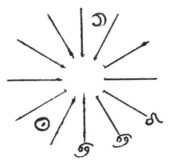

For instance, the Sun in the INVESTMENT-2nd tells us to try MONEY first and select the money-rulership of the houses holding Leo, the Moon and Cancer. Leo on the 6th is on the money-2nd for children, and the Moon in the 9th is in the money-by-INSURANCE-2nd for the death-8th. Cancer on both 4th and 5th is on the INHERITANCE-4th and also the father's money-2nd. We therefore say this event is the INVESTMENT of money in an INSURANCE policy, belonging to a child who IN-HERITED money from the father. All 4 points concur.

WHAT THE PLANETS REVEAL

The Sun

The Sun denotes an IMPORTANT event, one that will
not be postponed.   It will be a matter of the house
he is in, allied to a matter ruled by the house that
he rules & confirmed by the Ascendant or its ruler.
He is a SUPERIOR person having authority and rights
in the event when he rules or is in the First House.

Mars

Mars in the 1st, 4th, 10th or 8th denotes TROUBLE
and ACCIDENTS or VIOLENT INJURY, possibly DEATH: and
DANGER of DAMAGE to possessions. There may be BLOWS
and ARGUMENT or profanity, broken bones, and usually
an OPERATION if in any aspect with the Moon. He denotes INDEPENDENCE, rashness, DISOBEDIENCE, losses &
waste, fire and ARSON, and any THREAT, especially of
WAR.   He is active in INVESTIGATIONS and SEARCHES.

Saturn and Uranus

Saturn shows where the RESPONSIBILITY lies: he is
the MANAGER, denoting TIMING, delaying, obstructing,
limiting, planning & reaping in the event. He is an
older person, a PROBLEM, an official and The Reaper.

Uranus denotes unexpected, VEXATIOUS developments
when in the 1st House or conjunct the Sun or Moon, &
is likely to BREAK A LAW, flout the conventions, and
become party to UNBONDED RELATIONSHIPS, adoptions or
radical LEGISLATIVE involvements. He denotes circumstantial, ACCIDENTAL causes & INSTANTANEOUS results.
He is the IRRESISTIBLE FORCE, the only power capable
of meeting & defeating the IMMOVABLE BODY of Saturn.

Mercury

Mercury brings DOCUMENTS, contracts, agreements & communications in the case, possibility of MISTAKES, corrections, DECISIONS, examinations, and annoyance. He shows messages, VISITS, coming-&-going, appearing as a WITNESS or INFORMER, or an AGENT or go-between. He represents young people, relatives, small animals and those who SERVE (servants, teachers, nurses, the SECRETARIAL division of the Government, & so forth).

Jupiter

Jupiter denotes CEREMONIES, rituals, formalities, LEGALIZING moves; INSURANCE matters, CHARITY, church & college affairs, PROTECTION when angular; sports & TRAVEL, the stock market, publishers, EDUCATORS, the clergy, FOREIGN AFFAIRS, aliens, strangers, in-laws.

Neptune

Neptune denotes CHAOTIC conditions, DECEPTION and FRAUD, delusions, perversion, alcoholism & drugging, COLLAPSE, fainting, COMA, sabotage, subversion, KID-NAP, elopement, schemes, mysteries, DETENTION, plots & assassination, SUICIDE, disappearance, & an ALIAS. In the 6th, Neptune brings illness hard to diagnose.

Venus

Venus IMPROVES the event according to where Libra is found and the house she is in, & gives PROTECTION when angular. She denotes PEACEFUL MOVES, marrying, joining forces, RECONCILING, agreeing, fair dealing, entertaining and all SOCIAL affairs. She is OBEDIENT and even SUBSERVIENT, desirous of peace at any cost. She involves MONEY and POSSESSIONS, and some form of TRADITIONAL or customary development in the event.

The MOON for the activity

The Moon is the functioning force, the developing
power, the ACTIVE impulse, the CHANGING vibration, &
the SUBORDINATE agent operating at the Sun's behest.
She does not cause events but she does bring them to
fruition or not according to her condition as shown.

Increasing or Decreasing

Increasing in light (to become Full) the activity
GAINS IMPETUS, registers more & more, and stays with
the matter in hand, to slowly complete the activity.
Decreasing in light (to become New) the activity requires less time to finish and usually works faster.

Void of Course

When the Moon holds the highest degree-and-minute
she can make no applying aspect & is void of course:
she LETS THE MATTER DROP and takes no action. Whatever is ruled by the house she is in is "soon over &
done with" and all action now ceases. In the 7th, a
partnership is soon over; in the 11th, friendship or
membership is soon to end; in the 5th, a love-affair
will get nowhere; in the 6th, treatments are futile.

The Moon between planets

The Moon between two malefics, no matter how far
apart, is BESIEGED between evil forces that hold her
in bondage, greatly hampering her activity. A past
mistake leads to another now. If between benefics,
a good move in the past leads to another now. When
last over a malefic planet and next over a benefic,
a past mistake is in process of correction. If last
over a benefic and next over a malefic it shows that
a well-intentioned act in the past falls short now.

The Moon in Cancer or Leo

The Moon in Cancer denotes activity by one having an innate or natural right to act in the event. (She has a similar but lesser right in Pisces & Scorpio.) In Leo she describes one having conferred authority to act for a principal, but only for the time being. (See pages 193 to 215 for the Moon in other Signs.)

Dislike for the activity

The Moon in bad aspect to the ruler of the house she is in shows extreme dislike for the position in which she finds herself. She is not here by choice. She shows resentment if she rules or is in the 3rd.

The Angle of Distress

The Moon is always 6 houses after another (a 6th-House illness vibration) whose functioning she automatically upsets. When six houses after the one the Sun is in she denotes an untoward development in the activity that ricochets & somewhat upsets the event.

The Moon's Degree

In the first 3 degrees the Moon denotes embryonic activity still in the EARLY STAGES of formation. To 10 degrees, activity that is TAKING DEFINITE SHAPE & STARTING TO TAKE STEPS. In the middle of the Sign, it shows balanced & ESTABLISHED action. In the last 10 degrees, MATURE action especially regarding something long brewing. In the last 3 degrees she is in danger of being void of course: the activity is very FAR ADVANCED and ready (or preparing) to change now. In 29 degrees, the activity is somewhat unfortunate. A Critical Degree 0-13-26 of Cardinal Signs, 9-21 of Fixed Signs & 4-17 of Common Signs denotes a CRISIS.

Clues in reading an event

Public or Private

The 1st, 10th, 7th & 4th are out-in-the-open-ANGULAR houses. The Sun or Moon there signifies an event or the activity in an event taking place in public: but if intercepted, the event or the activity took place within a room or vehicle or enclosure or between two intercepting agencies, also coming to public notice.

In the 4th House & in the Sign on the 4th cusp the Sun or Moon signifies an event or activity occurring in a BUILDING or place of RESIDENCE. Exactly conjunct the 4th cusp, it happens directly on the THRESHOLD or at the doorway, gate or entrance of a residence or public building. In the 4th & in the Sign on the 5th, it occurs IN FRONT OF or NEAR a place of residence, etc. In the Sign on the 4th but in the 3rd House it happens BEHIND THE SCENES of a place of residence, etc. as a porch, garage or out-building.

In a SUCCEEDENT house (2nd, 5th, 8th and 11th) it denotes privacy & some secrecy; more quietly and involving taking a chance to some extent. Intercepted: in a private place or within an enclosure or railing there, somewhat set apart from the rest of the area.

In a CADENT house (3rd, 6th, 9th, 12th) the event or the activity is semi-private-and-semi-public such as prayers said in church, medical examinations, the airing of secrets in a letter, signatures and so on.

The Ascendant

The ruler of the 1st & the ruler of the house where the rising Sign belongs usually CONFIRM the reading.

Unfortunate

If the Sun, Leo, the Moon, Cancer or Ascendant-ruler
is in the 12th-of-misfortune or 8th-of-injury or the
Part of Fortune in the 12th, Pisces, 8th or Scorpio,
(Part of Mis-fortune) it shows an unfortunate event.
If 29 Taurus (the Weeping Sisters) is prominent, the
event or activity will give something to weep about.

Accidental or Deliberate

If Mars is afflicted in the 1st House (accidents) or
is in mutual reception with the ruler of the Ascendant or the Sun; or if Capricorn is on the 8th cusp &
the Ascendant is square a malefic, the event was due
to an accident. If the event is shown to be unfortunate and Mars is in the 11th House (circumstantial)
it happened accidentally because of circumstances at
the time and was neither intentional nor deliberate.

The event is deliberate & not accidental if the Sun
and Moon are in their own Signs (or in mutual reception with each other so that they may read as though
back in their own Signs) because they are intentionally working together.   If either of them conjuncts
Saturn or Neptune a plan or a scheme is part of it &
if they aspect both Saturn and Neptune or one of the
two & also the ruler of the 12th, then it is a plot.

Injury or Death

When the chart establishes misfortune or an accident
see if there is a malefic in the 4th denoting injury
that may require surgery or be permanently disabling
or fatal (see page 207).   The Moon and Mars in any
aspect whatsoever denotes a major or minor operation
which is more serious if Caput Algol in 24 Taurus is
conjunct or afflicting the Ascendant or its ruler.

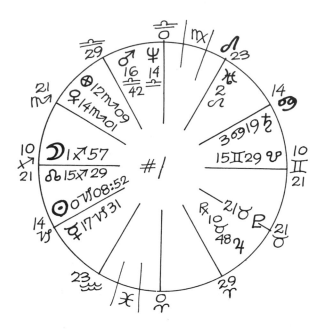

The Sun in the 1st House shows an event having to do
with a NEWCOMER who has just arrived, since he is in
0-degrees.   It is not a birth because Leo is not on
the 1st cusp (births) so it must be the ARRIVAL OF A
TRAVELER because Leo is on the travel-9th, & the 9th
Sign is rising and is the one the Moon is in.   Note
her exact trine to Uranus, co-ruler 3rd-of-VISITORS.

The Moon in the 12th combined with the Sign of going
from place to place shows activity related to travel
rather like EXILE as ruled by the 12th House, and it
is based on SEARCHING (her Sign on the 8th) to find
a HAVEN or peaceful home, because the 12th also signifies asylums & havens, and the Moon trines the 4th
cusp in 0-degrees (a new home): the ruler Mars is in
mutual reception with peace-loving Venus. Any mutual
reception with Mars fights for what the other wants.

ANSWER: The arrival of travelers to find a new home.

What the SIGNS & HOUSES reveal

ARIES and the 1st House

This is the house of BIRTH, arrivals, launchings, NEW BEGINNINGS, introductions, natural & INVOLUNTARY action, INDEPENDENCE, forward movements and CHANGES, always with the possibility of rashness & ACCIDENTS.

The activity of the Moon in Aries is PIONEERING & self-reliant, disdainful of danger, POSITIVE & often defiant, taking the offensive or assuming charge and desirous of acting without direction from others; it is fast-moving, pace-setting, personal and physical. In the Aries decanate of Leo and Sagittarius the action is tinged with these attributes and vibrations.

The persons represented are newcomers & arrivals, beginners, those making a personal debut & first appearance, the newborn; those involved in a hazardous undertaking or an accident; adventurers & pioneers.

The First House is more important than the others from the standpoint of CONFIRMATION. If the rising Sign is not Aries it belongs on another house which has a bearing on the case, as in the chart opposite. Where you find the rulers of these two houses, there will you find confirmation of something in the case.

Chart No. 1

This is the chart (from Ralph Kraum, astrologer), for THE LANDING OF THE PILGRIMS on Plymouth Rock, at 70 West Longitude, 41:58 North Latitude, on a Monday at 6:00 a.m. December 21, 1620 (New Style calendar). Note that Jupiter-the-traveler who rules the Ascendant lands in an Earth Sign in the chance-taking 5th.

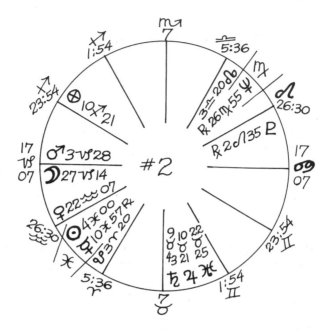

An event occurring in a PRIVATE room (Sun in the 2nd
and intercepted in bedroom-PISCES). Personal action
(Moon in the 1st), involving someone else (Cancer on
7th) who is an INTRUDER (Moon detrimented by Sign) &
whose activity now ceases (Moon now void of course).
It is UNFORTUNATE (Sun in Pisces, ruler 1st conjunct
ruler 12th, Mars in the same degree as the nodes and
also square (tragedy): Fortuna square co-ruler 8th);
& based on INJURY (Leo on the 8th: a malefic there).

It is MURDER (Leo on the 8th; the Reaper ruling the
1st & in the DELIBERATE Sign Taurus conjunct Jupiter
ruler assassination-12th who sesquares assassination
Neptune in the death-8th). The rising Sign belongs
on the 10th (EXECUTION when Scorpio is there and the
ruler Mars in the assassination-12th and last passed
over by the Moon whose last aspect was to Neptune).

ANSWER: It is the deliberate murder of an intruder.

TAURUS and the 2nd House

This is the house of SUBSTANCE, money, INVESTMENT
(not speculation, which is ruled by the 5th) movable
POSSESSIONS, personal property, securities, SAVINGS,
gifts to others, safe-deposit boxes & their contents
& evidence of the wherewithal necessary in the case;
SELF-PROTECTION and PERSONAL SECURITY to be guarded.

It rules HEREDITY, talents, CUSTOM and TRADITION,
PRECEDENT and the conventions, things done more than
once, therefore formulas & methods in personal use.

Being the injury-8th after the other-persons-7th,
it is the injury, surgery & death of OTHERS, and the
accidental damage and destruction of THEIR property.

The activity of the Moon in Taurus is DELIBERATE,
slow-moving, self-protective & self-interested; with
the same tinge in the Taurus decanate of Capricorn &
Virgo, and this is also true of the decanate rising.

The persons represented are owners of valuables &
savings, bankers, those protecting their own interests, involuntary destroyers of others and property.

Chart No. 2

This is the chart for the Hawkins killing of "the
other man" stated by several newspapers as occurring
at 4:00 a.m. Sunday, February 23, 1941, at Glendale,
California, 118:15 West, 34 North. (From Mr. H. S.)

Acquitted May 15, 1941. Venus angular PROTECTS &
in mutual reception with unexpected Uranus gets him
safely and unexpectedly out of what he got into. He
has protection also from the greater benefic Jupiter
angular, trine the Ascendant and conjunct the ruler.

A VISITOR behind the scenes of a building (Sun in 3d in Sign on 4th) probably a home (in dwelling-Cancer) who is NOT WELCOME (opposed by ruler of family-4th).

It is UNFORTUNATE (Fortuna in Scorpio and Sun & Moon square to ruler 12th) involves LEGAL BUSINESS ACTION (Moon in legalizing-9th in business Sign) upsets the family routine (Moon 6 houses after the home-4th she rules), and NOT BY CHOICE (Moon in bad aspect to the ruler of the house she is in; and Fortuna opposition Uranus-of-circumstances).

Leo on 5th involves COMMUNITY PROPERTY, selected because ruler 1st in Gemini in the 2nd shows dual ownership. Mars-of-machines in travel-Gemini in the 2nd describes a vehicle (automobile?) now taken by force (Mars square KIDNAP planet in joint-ownership-5th).

ANSWER: Legal repossession of a vehicle by stealth.

GEMINI and the 3rd House

This is the house of COMMUNICATION, conversation,
INFORMATION and its distribution, ADVERTISING, news,
messages, GOSSIP, letters, newspapers, magazines and
books, DOCUMENTS, schooling, INSTRUCTION, writing &
SIGNING; streets, TRANSPORTATION, traffic, neighbor-
hoods, visiting, COMING-&-GOING: the family secrets.
It is the house that is RELATED to something else or
CONTINGENT on an IMPERSONAL event requiring contact.

This is the house of the SHORTEST TIMING, brevity
and events that move swiftly & generally in the near
neighborhood. When the Sun is in the 3rd and in the
Sign on the 4th, the event occurs close to the home,
behind the scenes and often in an attached building.
Otherwise, it may happen NEARBY, perhaps in TRAFFIC.

The activity of the Moon in Gemini (or the Gemini
decanate of Libra & Aquarius) is IMPERSONAL & has to
do with a DOCUMENT, errors, CHANGES, communication &
information, VISITING or short trips and DELIVERIES.

The persons represented are relatives, visitors &
neighbors, tourists, gossips, messengers, witnesses,
reporters, notaries, teachers, students, & the black
sheep of the family or its "skeleton in the closet".

Chart No. 3

This chart from Mrs. R. L. V., astrologer, has to
do with the rude awakening of a couple when a deputy
seized the family car from the garage at one o'clock
sharp on the morning of June 27, 1934 at 118:15 West
Longitude and 34 North Latitude; afterward regained.

That he was armed & in possession of the required
papers is shown by Mars in the 2nd House, in Gemini.

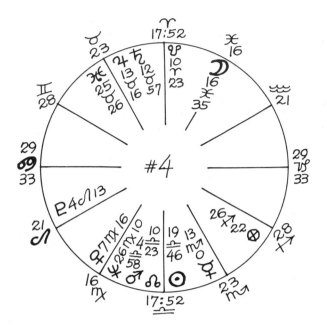

An event in a building (Sun in 4th in Sign on 4th) & having to do with MARRIAGE (Sun in marriage Sign and based on Leo on the 2nd of CUSTOM & TRADITION, where we find the marriage planet Venus). We select marriage because of confirmation of a wedding ceremony, the ruler of the 1st being conjunct the ritual-9th.

The activity of the Moon conjunct the legalizing-9th in Pisces of bondage in the domestic-Cancer decanate signifies marital bonds; a wedding ceremony based on Cancer on the 1st cusp (a new beginning, because the Sign is changing). To confirm a wedding ceremony we note Saturn ruler marriage-7th conjunct Jupiter ruler wedding-9th, & the Part of Fortune in Sagittarius the Sign of rituals. Fortuna's square to Neptune of MYSTERY in the travel-3rd shows a mysterious journey usually signifying an elopement (ruled by Neptune).

ANSWER: A wedding ceremony & probably an elopement.

CANCER and the 4th House

This is the house of DOMESTIC matters, individual and national; the HOME & national housing; the birth rate & the pre-natal period; INHERITANCE by descent, (not by gift as in the legacy-8th House). It rules DOMESTIC ECONOMICS and the FAMILY PURSE (and because it is the house of DISPLACEMENT it can be ROBBERY of the purse). It governs REAL ESTATE and property in general (farm, mine, well, garden, cemetery plots) & the place of PRESENT RESIDENCE (house, hotel, house-boat, trailer or tent, etc., which includes the womb before birth and the tomb after death), except 12th-House temporary or permanent residence-by-detention.

In INHERITANCE events, the 11th (being the death-8th of the family-4th) should reveal a death in the family by the presence there of Saturn, Uranus, Mars or the ruler of the 8th or 4th afflicted there. Neptune there sometimes means assassination or suicide. If it is money, the Sun, Jupiter, Venus, Fortuna, or Uranus (windfalls) or ruler 4th should be in the 2d. If real estate or family personal-property, the same or the Moon or ruler 2nd should be in the 4th House.

The activity of the Moon in Cancer (or the Cancer decanate of Scorpio & Pisces) is aimed at developing something for someone else and generally without receiving or expecting pay, usually with many CHANGES.

The persons represented are the family, an unborn child, workers on the home grounds; those on a jury.

Chart No. 4

This chart from Geraldine Davis, astrologer, told of the elopement-marriage of a very young couple, at 11:40:00 p.m. October 12, 1940 at Las Vegas, Nevada.

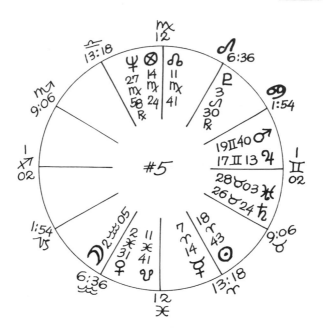

From the matters ruled by the 5th where we find the Sun, we select TAKING CHANCES - because the ruler of the 1st is conjunct the ruler of the 5th who is Mars (the daring planet) & the Sun is conjunct the mutual reception place of Mars.   These two conjunctions to Mars signify daring & the courage to pioneer alone. The rising Sign belongs on the 9th where we find Leo denoting EN ROUTE SOMEWHERE, which is chosen because it agrees with the Sign the 1st-ruler Jupiter is in. The activity is SELF-PROTECTIVE (Moon in the 2d) because of DANGER (Cancer on the 8th), and takes place by the side of a road (Moon conjunct the 3rd cusp).

It is UNFORTUNATE because the ruler of the 1st conjuncts the ruler of the 12th and squares Fortuna and signifies a DEATH (Cancer on 8th & Moon opposition a malefic there. Sun conjunct mutual-reception MARS).

ANSWER: A death, taking chances en route somewhere.

LEO and the 5th House

This is the house of everything SPECULATIVE as to the way it will turn out or the amount involved: the event has to do with TAKING CHANCES in some way, and involves speculation, GAMBLING, sports and contests, entertainment, theaters and pleasure resorts, love-affairs, the engagement period, COMMUNITY PROPERTY & things owned by two; joint bank-accounts; pregnancy.

This is the death-8th House for the 10th House of the mother, the president or other dignitary, or one being executed. In a chart with the Moon, Cancer or Leo on the 8th or 10th, the Sun and a malefic in the 5th indicate a death if confirmed by the 8th-ruler.

The activity of the Moon in Leo or the Leo decan-ate of Aries and Sagittarius is uneasy and insecure, acting under conferred authority from the Sun, often taking great chances and disclaiming responsibility.

The persons represented are gamblers, speculators & promoters, sportsmen, jockeys, contestants, lovers & children, entertainers & joint owners of anything.

Chart No. 5

An event occurring at 10:39 p.m. Pacific War Time April 8, 1942, Los Angeles, California. A newspaper account of a woman trying to reach home alone during a blackout, despite her fright. Running up a hilly street was too much for her and she suffered a heart attack, collapsed on the sidewalk, & died in a coma.

The ruler of the 1st conjunct Mars square Neptune denotes fright and also shows death in a coma. The Moon-ruler-8th opposition a malefic in the 8th & in the heart-Sign Leo may account for the heart-attack.

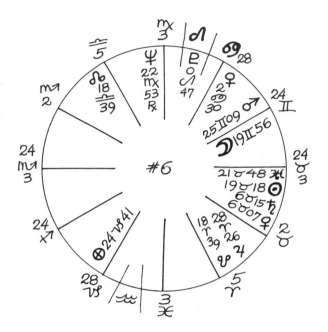

The Sun in the 6th shows MENTAL STRAIN because he is
conjunct a malefic. This is confirmed by Mars ruler
Ascendant in the mental Sign square chaotic Neptune.
It involves MAKING A CHOICE, which may offend public
policy because the Sun is in the Sign on the 7th and
at the same time afflicted by conjunction to Uranus.
It would be a destructive, irresponsible choice made
partly by the mental Mercury conjunct shrewd Saturn,
with both of them sesquare Neptune, planet of fraud.

The Moon in the 7th square Neptune is law-breaking &
the ruler of the 1st afflicted in the 8th destroys &
damages the possessions denoted by the Sun in Taurus
(ownership). Mars square ruler 4th destroys a home.

Since the Sun is in the money Sign, we will take Leo
& Cancer on the 9th to denote INSURANCE and the Moon
in Gemini to show activity with a document (policy?)

ANSWER: Property-destruction, to collect insurance.

VIRGO and the 6th House

This is the house of upsetting & DISTRESSING conditions and actions that usually affect the health &
all personal affairs.   The Sun here & afflicted denotes MENTAL STRAIN, based on something ruled by the
house Leo is on if confirmed by the Ascendant & its
ruler.   If the Sun in the 6th is in the Sign on the
7th and afflicted he is in a 12th-House unfortunate
relationship to the 7th and the event is inimical to
public welfare. If well aspected, the event is more
in the nature of a SERVICE (deed or ritual) to agree
with public welfare. It rules voluntary service for
the government or armed forces, CHOSEN WORK, nursing
and serving and CARE-TAKING of people & property for
self or others.   Being the natural house of digest-
ing and selecting-for-metabolizing the best, this is
the house of DISCRIMINATION and of VOLUNTARY CHOICE.

The activity of the Moon in Virgo or a Virgo decanate (Capricorn & Taurus) involves discriminating &
MAKING A CHOICE, deciding an issue in the jury-room,
taking care of the sick or of tenants & pet animals.

The persons represented are those giving service,
as a servant, orderly, waitress, tenant & caretaker,
watchdog, volunteer, nurse, practitioner or dentist.
(The 7th rules the physician & the 8th the surgeon.)

Chart No. 6

This test chart from Marge Zander, astrologer, is
set for an event occurring at 7:00 p.m. May 9, 1940,
118:15 West & 34 North, when an owner sought to free
himself from financial worry by burning his home and
belongings to collect the insurance. Note the ruler
of the 1st in mental-Gemini square Neptune-of-fraud,
from the 8th (ruling property-damage & destruction).

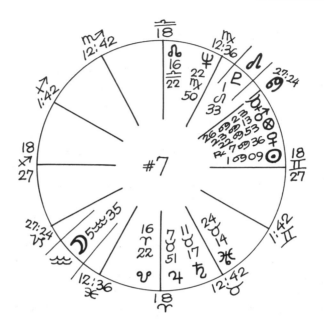

For the Sun in the 7th House we select a CONTRACT or
AGREEMENT, probably written, because document-Gemini
is on the cusp & signature-Mercury is in the 7th and
sextile alias-Neptune in the formal 9th House (where
the rising Sign belongs) denoting a formal signature
but in a different name.   The event has to do with
the home (Sun in Cancer, ruler 1st in home-4th), and
the event and activity in the event are based on the
same thing: danger and destruction held in abeyance,
because Leo is intercepted in the 8th and a malefic
is there, while Cancer is on the 8th and the Moon is
also intercepted.   The Moon in the 2nd opposing the
malefic in the 8th denotes a SELF-PROTECTIVE action
due to home-circumstances out of her control (she is
in Aquarius square the ruler of the 1st in the 4th).
It is an UNFORTUNATE necessity because Fortuna, Mars
ruler 4th, Mercury & Cancer are in the Pisces decan.

ANSWER: Self-protective agreement, to save the home.

LIBRA and the 7th House

This is the house of CONTRACTUAL and co-operative
events requiring AGREEMENT & SIGNATURE to inaugurate
or dissolve a legal measure.   A document figures in
the event if Mercury rules the Sign on or in the 7th
House; if he is in the 7th, a signature is involved.
It may be a contract, agreement, lease, note payable
or I.O.U., a power-of-attorney or proxy representing
a person empowered to act for another; and a treaty.

It rules PARTNERSHIP & its dissolution; MARRIAGE,
separation or DIVORCE, the marriage rate, common-law
unions; theft, LAWSUITS, open enmities, disputes and
INVASION or WAR; compromise, conciliation and PEACE.
It rules LIQUIDATION of estates, & legal handling of
8th-House bankruptcy; RECEIVERSHIP, repossession and
REMOVALS, and EXTRADITION of fugitives from justice.

The activity of the Moon in Libra or a Libra decanate (Aquarius & Gemini) is ON THE DEFENSIVE, seeking to protect, ease or help to effect harmony and a
peaceful solution; to UNITE as in partnership & marriage, through contracts or treaties & by agreement.

The persons represented are partners, spouses, an
agent, representative, creditor, receiver, executor,
lawyer, party to a contract, agreement or treaty; an
opponent or defendant; adversary in war, open enemy,
national enemy, thief, fugitive, healer & physician.

Chart No. 7

Time FRENCH SIGNED ARMISTICE at Forest of Compiegne,
6:50:00 p.m., June 22, 1940, at 3 East and 49 North.
The rising Sign belongs on the FORMAL 9th where Neptune-the-ALIAS is sextile Mercury-of-writing, giving
PROXY SIGNATURES of individuals for their countries.

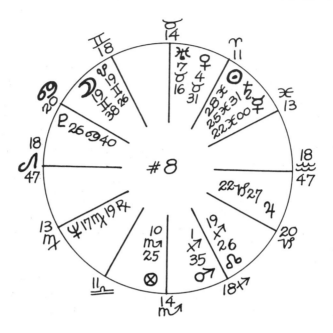

A most UNFORTUNATE event. The Sun is in the 8th and
in Pisces with Saturn & also with mutual-reception-
Neptune who is in a critical degree (page 189) while
Fortuna is the Part of Mis-fortune in Scorpio; & the
Moon rules the unfortunate-12th & is in the same degree as the nodes (a CASUALTY). The rising Sign belongs on the 5th whose ruler is in bad aspect with a
malefic in a critical degree in the 12th. It is bad
that there is no benefic angular to give protection,
while Leo is on the 1st (of danger of ACCIDENTS when
the Sun is in the danger-8th & squared by the Moon).

So many threats mean LARGE SCALE, & the Sun 8 houses
after Leo and the Moon last over Uranus-of-DISASTER
denote DEATH that is VIOLENT (Mars in the 4th) & accidental (Moon in the 11th) perhaps by an explosion,
(Mercury in the 8th semisquare to explosive-Uranus).

ANSWER: A large-scale disaster, with violent death.

SCORPIO and the 8th House

The 8th denotes INJURY, danger, SURGERY, DEATH, &
the death rate; toll taken as by TAXES, fees & tips,
DAMAGES, destruction, settlements & alimony.   It is
on a LARGE SCALE in a chart giving MANY indications.
It may involve WILLS & LEGACIES, goods of the dead &
gifts received; PUBLIC MONEYS: money by partnership,
marriage or a DOWRY; endowment; retirement premiums;
INVESTIGATION and SEARCH: books & safe-deposit boxes
now under EXAMINATION; it rules BANKRUPTCY & LOSSES.

In an INJURY or ACCIDENT, the ruler of the 1st in
the 4th or 8th afflicted by Mars or Saturn, & not in
mutual reception with Jupiter, shows someone KILLED.
Saturn in the 4th, death from WOUNDS; Neptune, death
in a coma, shock, unconsciousness; Uranus in the 4th
shows INSTANTANEOUS death; Mars, VIOLENT death, with
broken bones.   Jupiter-4th saves some as others die.

The activity of the Moon in Scorpio (or a Scorpio
decanate of Pisces & Cancer) tends to INVESTIGATE or
EXAMINE, to MEDDLE with or SEARCH anything private &
closed; any Moon-&-Mars aspect at all shows SURGERY.

The persons represented are those connected with
injury and death, such as a surgeon, coroner, under-
taker; one responsible in a fatal accident; killing,
as by a soldier, murderer or executioner; examiners,
researchers, detectives, investigators, accountants,
those bankrupt.   The Reaper, a destroyer & a corpse.

Chart No. 8

Explosion in Texas school, killing 400 pupils and
teachers: 3:05 p.m. March 18, 1937, 32 North 95 West
(chart from R.L.V.) Gas collected in the walls from
defective heating pipes.   (Gas is ruled by Neptune.)

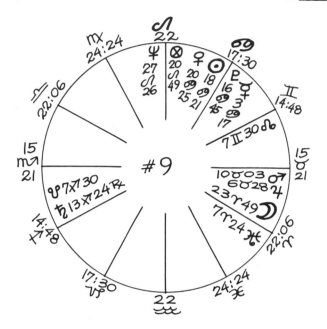

The Sun in the 9th House with Venus and Fortuna signifies a FORTUNATE event that is probably a CEREMONY
because the Moon rules the ceremonial-9th and is in
a formal-&-legalizing Sagittarian decanate, conjunct
Jupiter in the 6th House, denoting a formal SERVICE.
It goes against the family because the Moon was last
over Uranus-the-disruptive who rules the family-4th.

None of the significators are in the 7th House or in
Libra, so it is not a wedding.   They are not in the
2nd House or Sagittarius to denote insurance. It is
not a journey because the ruler of the Ascendant is
in a Fixed Sign, and the rising Sign belongs on the
8th where we find the coming-&-going Sign Gemini denoting only a visit. It is based on Leo on the 10th
with Neptune-the-ALIAS there and trined by the Moon,
suggesting a formal service regarding an alias-name.

ANSWER: A formal service having to do with the name.

SAGITTARIUS and the 9th House

This is the house of FORMALITY, and LEGALIZING by
a CEREMONY or ritual; parading; ETIQUETTE & CULTURE;
RELIGIOUS & ACADEMIC education; graduation, diplomas
and TITLE to property: INSURANCE and INDEMNITY paid
as recompense for 8th-House damage, injury or death.

It rules dissemination of KNOWLEDGE & circulation
of ideas as in TEACHING, preaching, WRITING, editing
and PUBLISHING, more formal and advanced than in the
3rd House which is just the opposite and elementary.

It rules moving from place to place as by TRAVEL,
voyages & journeys, including DREAMS (as journeys of
the mind). The Sun or Moon in the 9th shows an event
or the activity in an event en route somewhere.   In
an event concerning an absentee, if the ruler of the
1st or 9th is retrograde and especially conjunct the
9th cusp, it shows that the absent one is returning.

The activity of the Moon in Sagittarius or in the
Sagittarian decanate of Aries and Leo is LEGALIZING
and FORMAL; educational; moving from place to place.

The persons represented are those taking part in
a ceremony; paraders, travelers, absentees, aliens &
strangers, in-laws, grandchildren, churchmen & those
who pray; educators, writers, editors, insurance and
travel agents, members of a wedding that legalizes a
7th-House marriage or union; all those whose absence
upsets the family, being 6th after the domestic-4th.

Chart No. 9

This event is the LEGALIZING OF A CHANGE OF NAME,
at 2:15:00 p.m., July 10, 1928, at 34 North Latitude
and 118:15 West Longitude. (Mrs. T. E., astrologer)

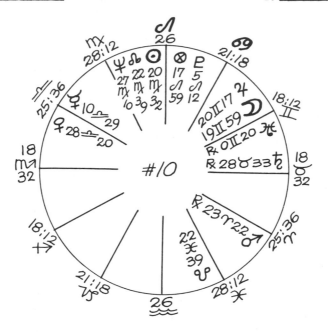

This is one of the easier charts to read: the Sun in
the 10th WITH A MALEFIC has to do with an EXECUTION,
because the 8th & 5th Houses are afflicted & Scorpio
is the rising Sign & square to Fortuna. The Moon in
the 8th denotes MURDER by square to Neptune and also
because there is no benefic angular to save, nor any
mutual reception to get him out of what he got into.
It is worse when the Ascendant is conjunct Serpentis
(one who pesters & is a terror to society), & Saturn
conjunct the Pleiades giving something to weep about
& also conjunct unavoidable-Uranus in the enemy-7th.
The rulers of the 1st & 7th have separated from some
relationship of the 5th and 12th Houses in the past,
so that the victim and the slayer are not strangers.
Leo on the 10th & Cancer on the 9th, with the rulers
square, involves business & insurance matters & much
wealth (Moon conjunct Jupiter-ruler-2d trine Venus).

ANSWER: Murder of a rich person for love and money.

CAPRICORN and the 10th House

This is the house of OFFICIAL BUSINESS as well as private & commercial enterprise, all conducted without feeling as a matter of EXPEDIENCY. It rules the Government, COURT & JUDGE, public policy or SECURITY MEASURES: a trial, conviction, sentence & EXECUTION. The Sun here with a malefic means unfavorable public notice & with an afflicted 8th or 5th, an EXECUTION.

It involves POSITION or standing in the community & thus REPUTATION, the good name (& the NAME itself) credit & discredit, honor & dishonor; EMPLOYMENT and CAREER. It brings more PUBLICITY than other angular houses; interceptions mean "not open to the public".

The activity of the Moon in Capricorn or a Capricorn decanate of Taurus or Virgo is patient, slow, & very conscientious, moving CAUTIOUSLY & according to circumstantial EXPEDIENCY - always with a good PLAN. In the 10th, she gives up part or all of her action.

The persons represented are officials, agents for the government, executioners, a social personage (or a social outcast), the Angel of Death for persons of the brethren-neighbor-3rd House; the mother; one who makes an appearance in public (unless intercepted) & one who comes to public notice; a judge, employer or business man; one unfortunate in 7th-House matters.

Chart #10

This event occurring at 10:15 a.m. Sept. 13, 1941 at 118:15 West, 34 North (chart from Mrs. H.S. based on newspaper account) is the murder of Mrs. Stricker who was beaten to death in her home & for her money, by an intruder who got safely away (note Venus ruler enemy-7th safe by Sign in the 12th House of hiding).

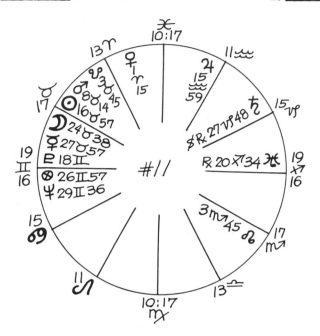

This is a harder chart to read: it is an UNFORTUNATE event with the Sun conjunct the 12th & in bad aspect to both benefics (square Jupiter, semisquare Venus): with the Moon in the 12th; and Neptune and Ascendant both in opposition to Uranus-the-irresistible force.

When Capricorn is on the 8th the Part of Peril gives a clue because exactly conjunct the Ascendant (RULE: the 1st plus the ruler of the 8th minus Saturn) & if in bad aspect to a malefic there is DANGER: (P) here is disastrous by bad aspect to Uranus-of-disasters; Saturn standing still in the 8th will destroy many, but Venus angular can save some while others perish.

The Moon conjunct Caput Algol makes it TERRIBLE, and Mercury ruler 1st in the 12th conjunct the Pleiades shows "something personal-&-physical to weep about".

ANSWER: A terrible disaster with great loss of life.

AQUARIUS and the 11th House

This is the house of CIRCUMSTANTIAL developments, due to the trend of affairs, not according to plan & expectation; a happenstance or CONTINGENCY allied to that which is ACCIDENTAL or fortuitous or by CHANCE. The Sun here denotes an event that was not planned.

It rules INTANGIBLE things not perceptible to the touch; hopes and wishes; the reason accounting for a special dream (being the 3rd after the 9th); friendship; and the intangible form following death (being the end-of-the-MATTER-4th after the death-8th), when the Being is no longer tangible but in ghostly form. It is the death-8th House for the 4th of the family.

It rules LARGE-SCALE events, universal in scope & often SCIENTIFIC, LEGISLATIVE or FREEING, and so OUT OF BOUNDS, unconventional & departing from the norm. It rules foster-relations, adoptions, memberships or UNBONDED RELATIONSHIPS, free love or universal love. Being the 2nd for the 10th it signifies the WAGES of employment, and gifts or MEDALS from the government.

The activity of the Moon in Aquarius or an Aquarian decanate (Gemini and Libra) is subject to CHANGE WITHOUT NOTICE: erratic, disruptive, and political.

The persons represented are friends, legislators, scientists, heroes, foster-relatives, free-thinkers, radicals, anarchists, communists, non-conformists or rebels, extremists, eccentrics, free-lovers, GHOSTS.

Chart No. 11

The ERUPTION OF MONT PELÉE, 7:50 a.m. May 8, 1902 at 61 West, 14:37 North. All 40,000 inhabitants die except a convict awaiting execution in a death cell.

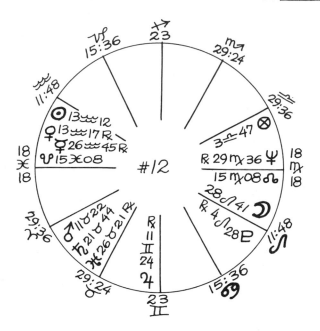

An UNFORTUNATE event (Sun in the 12th, the 12th Sign rising, the Part of Fortune conjunct Neptune), & may involve a death because the Sun conjuncts the ruler of the 8th and squares Mars and Saturn. The 12th is the death of a child (being 8th after the 5th, which is singled out for attention because Cancer is there & the ruler squares Uranus, the planet of disaster).

Venus-ruler-8th square Mars denotes a VIOLENT death.

It may be KIDNAP because the Sun in the kidnap-12th square daring-Mars is out-of-bounds in Aquarius; and the abducting-planet Neptune is an enemy in the 8th.

Leo on the service-6th is DISSERVICE when the Sun is in the 12th; confirmed by Mercury, natural 6th-ruler in the disservice-12th and square Uranus, a malefic.

ANSWER: A possible KIDNAP, involving violent death.

PISCES and the 12th House

This is the house of MISFORTUNE and MISADVENTURE, DETENTION, arrest, IMPRISONMENT, seclusion; MYSTERY, clandestine affairs, ambush, KIDNAP, assassination & SUICIDE, subversion, misinformation, obsession, hypnotism, gullibility, CONFINEMENT or hospitalization, estrangement, EXILE, regrettable acts, CRIME, behind the scenes hushed-up matters, SEANCES, self-undoing, CHARITY; slavery, BONDAGE, widowhood, sorrow, SHAME. When the Part of Fortune is in the 12th House or the 12th Sign Pisces it becomes the Part of Mis-fortune.

The activity of the Moon in Pisces or the Piscean decanate of Cancer or Scorpio is unfortunate to some extent if not entirely, unless in mutual reception & thus able to get out of the difficulty. There is an ENFORCED, subtle, patient BIDING-OF-TIME necessary & any error is due to being misinformed or uninformed; usually the activity resembles some form of BONDAGE.

The persons represented are SOCIAL MISFITS, those on relief, unfortunates, FAILURES, those living in a convent, monastery, cave; those under detention such as a lawbreaker, criminal, orphan, patient, slave or kidnap victim; those in sorrow; widows, complainers. Secret enemies, ambushers, kidnappers, assassins and suicides; scandalmongers, informers & liars. Clairvoyants & hypnotists; those who detain others, BORES & beggars, jailers, keepers, guards, enslavers & the police. Clandestine associates (especially if Venus or the ruler of the 7th is in the 12th). Drunkards.

Chart No. 12

Newspaper data: kidnap of 6-year-old San Bernardino, Calif. girl. 8:30 a.m. Feb. 2, 1942, 117-W & 34-N. Body found in desert next day: kidnapper not caught.

☆ ☆ ☆ ☆ ☆